Advance praise for
BE AN ANGEL

"These days, everyone seems to be searching for hope. In her powerful new book, *Be an Angel,* Roma Downey encourages readers to be willing to be used by God to fulfill a heavenly role like the angels do. This book will challenge your faith and inspire you to live each day to the fullest, bringing God's hope and love to a hurting world."

—CRAIG GROESCHEL, pastor of Life.Church
and author of *Dangerous Prayers*

"Hope, light, and encouragement . . . Roma Downey has done it again with *Be an Angel.* Get this book and let the love of God fill your heart page after page."

—KAREN KINGSBURY, #1 *New York Times*
bestselling author of *Someone Like You*
and the Baxters series

"Roma values kindness just as I do, and now her brand-new book, *Be an Angel,* has arrived to encourage and remind us to be more gentle and kind to one another. I truly believe we all need this book now, more than ever."

—SARAH FERGUSON, Duchess of York,
author, and humanitarian

"Our dear friend Roma Downey is a blessing to everyone who knows her, sharing God's love and hope wherever she goes. She has a kind and beautiful spirit, an enthusiasm for the things of God, and a desire to share her joy with everyone—all of which are reflected in her wonderful new devotional, *Be an Angel*."

—JOEL and VICTORIA OSTEEN

"We all need support and encouragement when we face challenges and difficulties, and others need us to be there for them at such times. The scriptures often cite that angels come to us in the appearance of a person who is there when needed, sometimes just for a moment, but making a meaningful difference. Angels are God's messengers of love, compassion, and support. Roma Downey's *Be an Angel* helps us to understand how we can all be angels for our families, friends, and people we don't know but whose needs we are aware of. *Be an Angel* is a blessing for all of us and for our world today, and would be a treasured gift for family and friends."

—CARDINAL SEÁN PATRICK O'MALLEY, OFM Cap., archbishop of Boston

"My beautiful friend Roma Downey has written another lovely book—one sure to encourage you to live with kindness, courage, joy, and faith. Her early experiences as an Irish lass raised in a loving home, filled with regular prayer and poetry, shaped her to be a writer of uncommon grace and elegance. I know you will love this book as much as I do."

—KAY WARREN, co-founder of Saddleback Church

"*Be an Angel* brings the power of godly love, the presence of godly comfort, and the path of godly blessings spoken by an angel: a messenger of God. Roma Downey is a present-day angel. I believe her book *Be an Angel* will be an oasis of encouragement in the desert days of your journey."

—BISHOP KENNETH C. ULMER, DMin, PhD, senior advisor to the president of Biola University

"Roma has written a loving guide to empower each of us to be messengers of wonderful, positive virtues of life. Reading it will enlighten you and in turn make you a shining light in a dark world. It makes all of us better!"

—BISHOP DALE C. BRONNER, founder and senior pastor of Word of Faith Family Worship Cathedral

"In *Be an Angel,* Roma Downey beautifully weaves personal stories and deep insights together with challenges, to help us connect with both ourselves and one another in more authentic ways."

—ARIANNA HUFFINGTON, founder
and CEO of Thrive Global

"Roma Downey played an angel but in real life she is filled with the beautiful light of God's presence. In *Be an Angel,* she empowers us with grace-filled truths that enable us to change the world with love, hope, mercy, and compassion. More than a must-read, without a doubt, a must-do!"

—SAMUEL RODRIGUEZ, senior pastor of
New Season Church, president of the National
Hispanic Christian Leadership Conference, author
of *Persevere with Power* and executive producer of
the films *Breakthrough* and *Flamin Hot*

"In her new book, *Be an Angel*, Roma Downey inspires readers to make their mark on the world through the virtues of courage, forgiveness, and hope. The book is timely and relevant, energizing and practical—a must-read for our day. You will find yourself encouraged, challenged, and lifted to a way of living that is deeply meaningful and satisfying. I highly recommend it."

—KEN FOREMAN, senior pastor of Cathedral of Faith

"Like so many, I first knew Roma through her on-screen character on *Touched by an Angel*. Years later I had the privilege to get to know the backstage Roma as a personal friend. *Be an Angel* is an extension of who Roma is in everyday life. She lives and writes to inspire us to live filled with hope, love, and faith. Roma invites us to find our light and to live our lives fully alive."

—ERWIN RAPHAEL MCMANUS, author of
The Genius of Jesus and founder of Mosaic

"Roma has long been the voice of a dear friend who lives out what it is like to be an angel presence for those around her. The words within the pages of *Be an Angel* will encourage you to reflect and act with loving wings throughout your days! Roma will capture your heart and set it in motion for others."

—ELISABETH HASSELBECK, *New York Times*
bestselling author and Emmy Award–winning
talk show host

BY ROMA DOWNEY

Box of Butterflies:
Discovering the Unexpected Blessings All Around Us

Unexpected Blessings:
90 Inspirations to Nourish Your Soul
and Open Your Heart

Love Is a Family (A Children's Story)

WITH MARK BURNETT

A Story of God and All of Us:
Companion to the Hit TV Miniseries The Bible

A Story of God and All of Us Reflections:
100 Daily Inspirations Based on the
Epic TV Miniseries The Bible

Son of God

BE AN ANGEL

BE AN ANGEL

Devotions to
Inspire and
Encourage Love
and Light
Along the Way

ROMA DOWNEY

CONVERGENT

NEW YORK

Library of Congress Cataloging-in-Publication Data
Names: Downey, Roma, 1960- author.
Title: Be an angel / Roma Downey.
Description: New York: Convergent, 2023.
Identifiers: LCCN 2022036786 (print) | LCCN 2022036787 (ebook)
| ISBN 9780593444023 (hardcover) | ISBN 9780593444030 (ebook)
Subjects: LCSH: Kindness—Religious aspects—Christianity—Quotations,
maxims, etc. | Affirmations. | Angels—Miscellania.
Classification: LCC BV4647.K5 D69 2023 (print) | LCC BV4647.K5 (ebook)
| DDC 241/.4—dc23/eng/20220929
LC record available at https://lccn.loc.gov/2022036786
LC ebook record available at https://lccn.loc.gov/2022036787

Printed in the United States of America on acid-free paper

crownpublishing.com

1st Printing

First Edition

Book design by Jo Anne Metsch

In memory of my parents,
Maureen O'Reilly and Paddy Downey,
who taught me the importance of kindness
and led by example,
and my "adopted mother" and former co-star,
Della Reese, who taught me how to be an angel
and trust my wings.

Contents

COURAGE

FORGIVENESS

HOPE

FAITH

GRATITUDE

FRIENDSHIP

TRUST

GRACE

LOSS

ENCOURAGEMENT

JOY

CHANGE

BE AN ANGEL

1

Start at the Very Beginning

*Thinking about the beauty of the angelic world gives a
glimpse of the beauty and greatness of God.*

SERGE-THOMAS BONINO[1]

*W*hat does it mean to be an angel?

I've thought about this question a lot, especially since I had the privilege of playing one on television for almost ten years. I loved being Monica, the kindhearted angel on the hit show *Touched by an Angel.* Some years later, I produced *The Bible,* an epic miniseries that required casting and costuming a heavenly host. My work on these projects compelled me to study angels—their work, their messages, their connection to God and people. I'm thrilled to share with you some of what I've experienced and learned.

The simplest definition of *angel* is "a messenger, especially of God."[2] In the nearly three hundred references to angels in the Bible, we find angels speaking the words of God, bringing the news of God, and doing the work of God. Angels repeatedly told people not to fear. They reminded people of God's nearness. They brought hope and light.

Angels defend and protect us, mainly from our enemies but sometimes from ourselves. They guide and direct us when we're lost or confused. Angels speak the truth: God loves us and we are *never* alone. This message brings healing and restoration; every hurt done to us and every hurt we have done can be forgiven.

Oh, how I need to hear this! How we *all* need to hear this!

Over the years, because of my role on TV, people often mistook me for an actual angel. They projected their feelings about the show onto me and my co-star Della Reese. I sometimes wanted to explain, "I'm just a person—a human!"

There was one incident at a children's hospital I was visiting. I walked by a room filled with sadness. A young child had passed away, and heartbreaking grief poured out of the room with the remaining family members. The bereft mother saw me, recognized me from TV, grabbed me in an embrace, and began weeping.

"Monica," she sobbed. "I prayed that God would send me an angel, and here you are."

I honestly didn't know what to say. She needed an angel, and I was just an actress in the hallway of a hospital. I held her close and quietly prayed for her and her loved ones. After a while, she thanked me, then returned to join her family. I left feeling so very sad.

Later that night, I recounted the story to Della. "She thought God sent me," I lamented. "She thought I was an angel."

My wise, wonderful friend replied, "Baby girl, who's to say God didn't send you to be there?"

Della taught me that if we're going to be used by God, we need to let go of our expectations and get out of the way. Since then, I have tried to do that very thing, never pretending to be anything I'm not but simply holding a loving space for others.

Della also helped me understand that a person who speaks the truth of God or performs a mission for Him fulfills a heavenly role like the angels do. That's why we call a woman like Mother Teresa an angel of mercy. She was a human, just like us, but she chose to be like an angel in how she lived. That's how I want to live.

The words of angel expert Serge-Thomas Bonino that you read at the opening of this entry remind us that angels give us a glimpse into the beauty and greatness of God. What if you and I lived so that people saw more of His beauty and greatness through us? What if we lived in such a way that kindness, truth, and love defined us? I believe it's possible for us to be like angels in bringing God's message to Earth.

That's why I chose to write this book. I want to encourage you, as I've been encouraged, to live like an angel on Earth. I want you to join me in speaking words of hope to a hurting world, bringing light into darkness.

At the end of each chapter, there will be a "Be an Angel" section where I'll invite you to put what you've read into practice. Some of these suggestions will be exciting and fun; others may challenge you. Some will involve things to ponder; others will invite you to action. I pray each inspires you to give or receive a glimpse of God's beauty and greatness. Are you ready to get started? If so, let's begin!

Be an Angel

Sometimes gentle and soothing words can be as comforting as a warm breeze. Today, why not take a moment to write a note to someone who is going through a tough season and let them know you're thinking of them? Your loving words and the time you took to reach out will remind them they are loved and never alone.

Kindness

2

Stay Golden

In everything, do to others what you would
have them do to you, for this sums up the
Law and the Prophets.

MATTHEW 7:12

I'm so grateful for the special relationship God
has given me with Reilly, my beautiful daughter.
From the moment I first held Reilly in my arms, God
opened the door to a love stronger and deeper than I'd
ever imagined. I cherished the times we spent during
her early years, building snowmen in the winter and
sandcastles in the summer. We constructed elaborate
forts for stuffed animals, with whom we also reenacted
our favorite movies. As Reilly grew, I celebrated her
accomplishments and helped her during heartache.
Whatever we're doing, wherever we are, I love being
her mom.

When Reilly hit adolescence, she sometimes had
questions about school, friends, or teenage drama. As
part of the theater program at school, she and her class-

mates had to navigate getting—or not getting—the roles they wanted.

"I don't know what to do, Mom," she'd lament.

"What would you want someone else to do in this situation?" I'd usually respond. "How would you feel if you were in the other person's place?"

"My feelings would be hurt," she might reply, or "It was really disappointing to make it through to the final callback and not get the part."

Reilly and I had important talks about rejection. In the acting world, someone will always have the happy feeling (*I got the part!*), while someone else will have the hard feeling (*I didn't land the role*). I wanted her to know that, even though rejection is a big part of the entertainment world, she could reframe her thoughts, putting herself in the place of others, and deliberately respond with kindness.

In these conversations, I pointed Reilly back to the Golden Rule. The gospel of Matthew records how Jesus articulated this principle: "Do to others what you would have them do to you" (7:12). A version of this simple maxim can be found in almost every culture around the globe.

Over the years, I spent time cultivating Golden-Rule kindness with Reilly. We'd discuss whether she needed to do something *for* someone or show compassion and forgiveness *to* someone. Times when Reilly or I needed to ask for forgiveness from someone else arose too. Pondering the Golden Rule almost always led us to the best next step, whether that was a decision to make or an action to take. When my daughter and I chose to align ourselves with the words of Jesus, we brought more of His love and light to the world, just like His heavenly angels do when they touch human lives.

How do you respond to this, dear one? Do you regularly practice the Golden Rule? If so, keep going! If not or if your answer is "Sometimes but not always" (like it is for most of us!), today is a great day to start reflecting God's character of love, kindness, and respect for all people. You can be like an angel on Earth by staying golden.

Be an Angel

Pure gold is beautiful and valuable. Living a Golden-Rule life is lovely and precious too. Take a deep breath and think about the last time you had a disagreement with someone you love. Consider how the situation might have changed if *you* had changed. Even if the other person was more in the wrong, how might your practicing the Golden Rule have altered your conflict? Jot a few thoughts down in a journal and then talk with the Lord about it in prayer. You'll glow more golden as you do.

3

Exceed Expectations

Unexpected kindness is the most powerful, least costly,
and most underrated agent of human change.

BOB KERREY

ob Kerrey grew up in Lincoln, Nebraska, during the 1940s and '50s. Nothing prepared him for what he witnessed—and participated in—as a Navy SEAL during the Vietnam War. Wounded and permanently disabled during his tour of duty, Kerrey received an unexpected gift: compassion for those who suffer and an appreciation for the capacity of leaders to change lives. He became a leader to do just that. His words about kindness resonate powerfully because his experience could have turned him cold and embittered.

In a world that expects otherwise, kindness sets us apart. Unexpected kindness disarms people and de-escalates conflict. To an often hurting and angry world, kindness reveals a patient and merciful God, a God who loves. Like Bob Kerrey, I believe kindness is the most potent, the least expensive, and an all-too-often underestimated agent of change.

I've learned that between every stimulus and response lies a space and, in that space, we get to choose.
Kindness often involves *not* reacting to something
quickly. Difficult? Yes. Impossible? No! We can train
ourselves to respond with kindness when someone
might expect defensiveness. We can train ourselves to
choose compassion when anger feels more natural. We
don't have to do what's expected. We can rise above
because we're created by God for love, not hate. Isn't
that wonderful?

Over the last couple of years, I've learned about
kindness in some new ways. Kindness has always been
important to me, but I still had room to grow. God
placed His hand on a particular area of my life—my
response to criticism—and helped me develop unexpected kindness. Instead of responding with defensiveness, I've been deliberately trying to cultivate a gracious
heart when someone gives me feedback. I think this is
especially important in our families, where we're both
our best and our worst selves. If we lean in and listen,
our family can provide such insight for us. Rather than
dismissing criticism or justifying why I did something,
I now try to respond with "Thank you for sharing this
with me and giving me this feedback."

I can think through what that person brought to my
attention and become better as a result. I can apologize
for how I hurt someone. I can respond to criticism

with kindness. This has transformed not only me but also the people around me. That's what kindness does: It changes things. It changes people.

The Bible tells us that God created angels as "ministering spirits" (Hebrews 1:14). They help and serve because that is what God created them to do. Like the angels, we fulfill what we were made to do when we reflect God's character, including His kindness. Luke 6:35 tells us that God shows kindness to the ungrateful, to those who respond with cruelty rather than kindness. In other words, God's kindness far exceeds expectations. Dear one, let's go and do likewise.

Be an Angel

This week, when we feel angry or defensive, let's respond graciously rather than react quickly. If someone offers feedback, let's receive it patiently and give it attention. Unexpected kindness will make healthy change and forward movement possible. Together, let's watch the difference kindness makes.

4

Listen to Their Stories

Kindness begins with the
understanding that we all struggle.
attributed to CHARLES GLASSMAN

I have such fond memories of Christmas morning in Derry City, my hometown in Northern
Ireland. Children of all ages would spill out of the
neatly lined row houses, excited to show one another
the treasures Santa brought. We'd share our joys and
our toys, playing until Christmas dinner.

One year when I was still quite young, a neighbor
girl brought out the twin dolls she'd received. After
eyeing them suspiciously, I bolted home, raced up the
rickety staircase to our attic, and searched high and low.
I knew it! My twin dolls—the very same dolls I'd
dressed up, cared for, and loved—were nowhere to be
found.

Marching downstairs, filled with childish indigna-
tion, I found my mother.

"That wee girl has *my* dolls. She said Santa brought
them for her."

Mom took my hands kindly.

"Santa can only do so much, Roma girl. Sometimes parents have to supplement. That little girl's father died this year, and their family doesn't have much. We gave them your old dolls."

My demeanor instantly changed. My mother and father had always taught me to have a generous heart. They reminded me that God was generous with us and that we honored Him by treating others with kindness and compassion. That day, I learned (though it took me years of growing up to grasp) that things aren't always what they seem. Everyone has a story; everyone hurts.

I so admire how my mom handled this situation. She didn't spoil the magic of Christmas, for me or for this little neighbor girl, giving away "the truth" about Santa. Still, Mom taught me an essential lesson. She helped me embrace the power of kindness for those who struggle—in other words, for us all.

Historical records detail the incredible generosity of Saint Nicholas, around whom the legend of Santa Claus originated. Tradition tells us that Nicholas heard about the troubles of others, then gave lavishly and lovingly. A man of deep faith in God, Nicholas blessed others because he knew the Blessed One (see 1 Timothy 6:15). His kindness became so renowned that, around the world, people still revere Nicholas as a saint.[3]

Am I renowned for kindness? I'd like to be, so I've chosen to live with kindness always in mind. Bottom line, we don't know who might be caring for aging parents or watching a child slide deeper into addiction. We don't know which colleague or neighbor hasn't slept well, is waiting for those test results, or is hoping not to hear from the credit agency.

People may or may not tell us their stories, but we can always be listening. We can attune ourselves to those around us, showing kindness because we know that everyone struggles. Whether people presently find themselves in paradise or the pit, showing love is always our best choice. Let's listen for the untold stories today and treat everyone with kindness.

Be an Angel

In the Czech Republic, the celebration of Saint Nicholas Day traditionally includes three costumed characters: Nicholas, an angel (representing good), and the devil (representing evil). In Prague, these three speak to children about their choices—good and bad—over the past year.[4] I wonder what we'd say if an angel asked about our choices over the past year. What changes might we want to make to be more like Saint Nicholas: generous and kind? Let's start making one change today.

5

Go Beyond

Love your enemies! Do good to them. . . .
Then your reward from heaven will be very
great, and you will truly be acting as children of the Most High, for he is kind to
those who are unthankful and wicked.

LUKE 6:35 (NLT)

ecause I grew up during a war, I read this verse and think of gunshots and petrol bombs, riots and hatred. The Troubles—also called the Northern Ireland conflict—erupted because people saw one another as enemies. Others may think of Luke 6:35 metaphorically, but I remember what marked my childhood: actual violence and enmity.

The priests in my parish echoed what Jesus taught: Love your enemies. They reminded us that everyone wanted justice but that hatred wouldn't bring our country peace. I was incredibly fortunate to be led by godly people who lived these truths out, including Father Edward Daly. He is best known for the famous Bloody Sunday photo in which he waves a white handkerchief splattered with the blood of a young man he's helping usher out of the war zone. Father Daly, who eventually became the bishop of Derry, led our community with the clear teaching of Jesus to love, not hate.

At home, my father reinforced this truth by word and example. He showed me how to live in love, even when people around me spewed venom. Paddy Downey taught me and my brother to pray for the people who screamed obscenities during riots. He taught us, by example, to bless those who cursed others.

To this day, I live by the examples with which I was raised at home and at church. Together, my husband, Mark, and I passed the importance of kindness—love in action—on to our children as well. We taught Reilly, James, and Cameron that kindness isn't always easy but that practicing it makes a big difference. The more we bless instead of curse, the easier it becomes to extend kindness to our enemies.

For instance, when someone snipes at me or belittles my work on social media, I practice noticing that person's pain. I pray about whatever might have motivated them to attack me. When I turn my feelings into a prayer, it begins a shift in my perspective. Again, this isn't always easy. I have found, however, that kindness to people who are unkind to me flows more naturally when I practice it regularly.

What do you think about intentionally choosing kindness? Have you seen how this shifts the tide in you, even if the other person doesn't change? Sometimes we want our actions to transform the "other guy." And it *would* be wonderful if our kindness changed everything instantly. But, as Jesus' words remind us, some people will choose to be ungrateful. Some people will even choose to be wicked. Those who threw bombs into buildings, killing innocent people during the Troubles, acted wickedly. But they, too, were created in God's image; I can pray for them rather than cursing them.

The outcome isn't immediate perfection in me or around me, but consistent change over time does occur. Leading with kindness disarms others and opens a door of love. With me, will you open your heart in compassion today?

Be an Angel

Angels sometimes came to Earth with fanfare, other times quietly. Choosing to be a messenger of God's love doesn't have to be big and operatic. Small acts of kindness can ripple out in huge ways. What would it be like if you led with compassion, starting with small shifts in your thinking? Maybe you could begin with a prayer for the last person who sniped at you.

Love

6

Learn to Love

No one is born hating another person because of the color of his skin, or his background, or his religion. People must learn to hate, and if they can learn to hate, they can be taught to love, for love comes more naturally to the human heart than its opposite.

NELSON MANDELA, *Long Walk to Freedom*

*N*elson Mandela grew up in a nation saturated with hate. Under the wicked apartheid system, which institutionalized racial discrimination, he was tried several times and imprisoned for more than twenty-seven years. Despite constant provocation, Mandela inspired others to oppose oppression and deprivation with wisdom rather than with knee-jerk retaliation. He lived the truth that love and hate are *choices.*

Perhaps Mandela's words move me so deeply because I also grew up in a country torn by hate. Segregation and discrimination infected Derry as the Troubles raged. The struggle spanned thirty years as it pitted my people against one another.

The River Foyle didn't simply divide our landscape in Derry; it also separated the hearts of its citizens. People on opposite sides of the river didn't associate, shop at the same stores, or go to the same schools. Children grew up hearing their parents speak hatefully about "those people."

As a little girl walking home from school, I would be detoured away from buildings under bomb threats. I observed hatred firsthand as riots broke out. There are few words to describe the terror of being caught in a riot. The imminent danger—the bricks, rocks, and bottles thrown by raging neighbors—horrified me quite enough. But the venomous words, the expressions of loathing and disgust on people's faces—these were almost worse.

I'm so grateful that at home I learned something entirely different. My dad modeled love, compassion, and kindness no matter what the Troubles brought to our community. He told me that love was a choice, and I have lived in that truth ever since. I deliberately rejected hate and bitterness then; I continue to do so now.

Choosing to love aligns us with the heart of God. God Himself *is* love, so making the daily decision to spurn hate and practice love brings me closer to Him. Genesis 1:27 declares that God created every human being in His image. This means we are made to love, not hate. That is why Mandela said love comes more naturally to our hearts.

In the Bible, angels sometimes arrived during times of intense conflict. In one instance, an angel used a donkey to stop a man who'd been hired to curse God's people. The angel would not allow Balaam to spread hate; instead, God turned Balaam's words into blessing (see Numbers 22–24).

In our day, angels might not use animals to stop people from posting a mean social media rant or speaking ungracious words at a party, but we can live as messengers of God by making daily choices to reject hate and practice love. No matter what we were raised to believe, we can learn to love and model compassion for others. Mandela's words affirm that none of us is too far gone. Together, let's live in love.

Be an Angel

Pause for a moment to take stock of what your life is currently teaching the people around you. Are your words—at home, at work, online—filled with love or with something else? Are there ways in which you might want to change? Today is a wonderful day to commit anew to love.

7

Make Someone Feel

I've learned that people will forget what you said,
people will forget what you did, but people will never
forget how you made them feel.

MAYA ANGELOU

I first met Maya Angelou on the *Touched by an Angel* set. She guest starred in a gripping episode about love and loss. I would have enjoyed simply sharing the screen with Maya, but because of my close relationship with Della Reese, I received a far greater blessing.

"You know, this is my baby girl," Della informed Maya.

"Well, I guess that makes me your auntie," Maya immediately responded.

And so Maya took me in as one of her very own. I will never forget being in her beautiful North Carolina home, talking and laughing into the night.

"Would you care to have me read anything?" she asked.

"Oh yes, anything," I replied.

As she began to read, in the quiet half-light of her kitchen, time stood still. Listening to Maya recite her poem "Still I Rise" will be imprinted on my heart forever, as will the time I brought a camera crew to film an interview with Maya about *The Bible* miniseries.

Maya had graciously agreed to help promote the show, and I assembled a team to record the segment at her home. They were a young bunch, just kids really. Not wanting to disturb Maya any more than we had to, I arranged for box lunches to be delivered for me and the crew. As we set up in a corner of the garden for our lunch break, Maya burst outside.

"What are you doing?"

(Insert general stammering and shrugging from the twentysomethings.) "Eating," someone offered sheepishly.

"And what is wrong with my dining table?"

Maya laughed her irresistible laugh and insisted that we join her inside for lunch. For the next hour, she hosted us around her table, kindly and deliberately asking every single member of the crew about themselves. Under Maya's loving gaze and rapt attention, the young cameramen sat up taller. The sound techs laughed more readily and looked one another in the eye. Maya gave each individual dignity, and it changed all of us. I don't remember what she said to each person, but I remember how she made us feel.

Maya saw people. She really *saw* them. She uplifted everyone around her. I've chosen to live that way, following her example.

How many conversations with a friend can you recite word for word? I'm guessing not that many. But you remember what it felt like when you lost your job or loved one and that friend was there for you, reminding you that you aren't alone. How many sermons can you remember perfectly? Probably none! But you likely recall when the pastor officiated your wedding or helped you through that family crisis. In those moments, you felt the presence of God through other people, His angel-like messengers.

We sometimes believe we need to have the right words or the right advice. Most of the time, we simply need to *be present with someone,* helping them connect with God's peace and hope. That's why Maya's words that started this chapter ring so true. What will you do with this truth? How will you make others feel?

Be an Angel

How can you make someone feel valued today? Perhaps you could pick up their favorite coffee or tea and ask the barista to write "You are loved" on the cup. Maybe you could leave a voicemail for a friend, singing their favorite song (even if you can't carry a tune in a bucket, this will be unforgettable). There are thousands of small ways you can act like an angel and make someone feel as special as God created them to be.

8

Cast a Stone

I alone cannot change the world, but I can cast a stone
across the water to create many ripples.
commonly attributed to MOTHER TERESA

*I*n 1929, an eighteen-year-old Albanian woman named Anjezë Bojaxhiu moved to India. Captivated by the lives of missionaries, their devotion to God, and their love for others, Bojaxhiu entered a convent. She taught faithfully for seventeen years before experiencing what she described as a "call within a call."[5] Responding to God, she served the poorest of the poor people while living among them. When Bojaxhiu took her final vows, she received the title Mother Teresa.

Mother Teresa didn't set out to change the world; she chose to love one person at a time. She placed a pillow under the head of one suffering woman. She mopped the brow of one feverish man. She wiped away the tears of another and fed a hungry child. She cast one stone at a time into the sea of humanity. Love rippled outward.

Mother Teresa saw the face of Jesus in everyone she served. She wasn't perfect, as she readily confessed, but she loved deeply and freely. Her love inspired people to cast their own stones into the sea of suffering and need. Together, those ripples created a powerful force of change.

I've always felt inspired by Mother Teresa. And when I had the opportunity to work with Operation Smile, an amazing nonprofit organization that offers craniofacial surgeries to those who could never afford the procedure, I felt like I was casting my own stone of love. I watched the ripples radiate outward, changing one child's life—giving one child a face, a smile, words rather than silence. But the love didn't stop there. A child's surgery changed a mother, then a family, then a community.

When Mark and I took our children on Operation Smile missions with us, we wanted to create a legacy of love, change, and kindness in our family. Our kids introduced their classmates to Operation Smile, and the group committed to raising the money for one surgery. What a practical way to see and *be* the change! As each child gave their donation, love rippled outward.

I could have missed all of this. On my first trip with Operation Smile, I went to Vietnam, where the enormous need overwhelmed me. We had funds for maybe fifty surgeries, but two hundred people had signed up. "I can't help them all," I cried out to God. His response: *But you can help these. These fifty matter, and you are part of My love for them.* On a much smaller scale but in a similar way, I learned what Mother Teresa did: I cannot change the world, but I can cast a stone of love. So can you, dear one. So can you.

Be an Angel

A legacy of love starts with the first pebble dropped. What stone can you cast across the water this week? Perhaps you can send flowers to someone battling an illness or deliver a meal for someone who recently lost a loved one. Can you support a charity or volunteer or—better yet—do both? Let's cast a stone of love and watch the ripples grow.

9

Let Them Know

Love each other. Just as I have loved you,
you should love each other. Your love for
one another will prove to the world that
you are my disciples.

JOHN 13:34–35 (NLT)

As a schoolgirl, I learned a song written by a Chicago priest during the civil rights movement. Father Peter Scholtes was leading a youth choir and looking for music appropriate for a series of interracial events. When he couldn't find a song, he wrote the now-iconic hymn "They'll Know We Are Christians by Our Love" in one day.[6] Father Scholtes's simple song became a favorite of mine and an anthem for Christ followers around the world.

Fast-forward half a century to when I produced *A.D.: The Bible Continues* with my husband, Mark. For the soundtrack, we had the opportunity to work with amazing recording artists, including the Australian duo For King and Country, who brought Father Scholtes's hymn to life with their powerful vocals and drum section. Their version of "They'll Know We Are Christians by Our Love" is a call to action, exactly like Jesus' words in John 13.

You are one in My Spirit, Jesus told His disciples. *Your love proves that to the world. Love because I have loved. Love as I have loved.*

I have a strong sense that "They'll Know We Are Christians by Our Love" is every bit for this moment in history as it was for other periods of unrest, division, and enmity. Jesus called His followers to love in a radical way, and Father Scholtes's words reflect this: "We'll guard each other's dignity and save each other's pride."[7] In other words, we cannot simply *say* we love; we need to *act* consistent with love. As my dad always said, "Love is a verb."

How we love reveals who we are and what we stand for. How we love consistently aligns us with Jesus . . . or not. There's no integrity in sitting in church on Sunday singing about God's love while hating people the rest of the week.

I've received some rather hurtful comments online. How I respond to people on social media—even strangers attacking my work or convictions—sends a message to everyone in my sphere of influence. Will the world know I'm a Christian by my love? I pray it will be so, and I make choices accordingly. I *love* because Jesus loves me. I don't love perfectly, like He does, but my everyday commitment to love—as an action verb!—keeps me close to God.

When Mark and I traveled to promote both *The Bible* and *A.D.: The Bible Continues,* we received invitations to share about our journey at many churches. In so many congregations, we knew people were Christians by their love. Sadly, some churches embodied a religious spirit of judgment and condemnation. This grieved my heart, and I believe it grieves God's too. In those instances, I took seriously my role as one of God's messengers of love and truth. It wasn't always easy, but walking in the footsteps of Love never has been, has it?

Dear one, what does your love currently reveal to the world? Are there ways God might be inviting you to love deeper, truer, or stronger? Let the world know what you stand for by your love—*His* love.

Be an Angel

Find a recording or video of "They'll Know We Are Christians by Our Love" online. Consider the lyrics thoughtfully. Write down any words God highlights for you and what He might want you to do in response.

Courage

10

Armor Up!

If your valley is full of foes, raise your sights
to the hills and see the holy angels of God
arrayed for battle on your behalf.

BILLY GRAHAM, *Angels*

*M*ark and I relished working with an amazing team of more than forty pastors, theologians, historians, and Hollywood colleagues to bring *The Bible* to television. Amazingly, more than one hundred million people have tuned in.[8] Mark and I knew the world would be watching, and we wanted to get things right! We had the chance to help people understand who God is, so we meticulously attended to every detail, eager to spread His gospel message of love and redemption.

When it came time to costume the angels, we ran into some unexpected challenges. We originally styled them in white garments and ethereal lighting, with flowing fabric and hair. To be honest, in the grittiness of our first-century Middle Eastern–inspired set, this looked ridiculous. Something had to change.

After spending more time investigating how angels looked, spoke to humans, and interacted with them, we decided to give viewers a glimpse of another role of God's messengers: the warrior host of heaven. Arrayed in armor, battle-scarred, and ready for action, these angels came to Earth as defenders and protectors. We see this angelic role in 2 Kings, when the enemies of God encircled His prophet Elisha:

> When the servant of the man of God got up and went out early the next morning, an army with horses and chariots had surrounded the city. "Oh no, my lord! What shall we do?" the servant asked.
>
> "Don't be afraid," the prophet answered. "Those who are with us are more than those who are with them."
>
> And Elisha prayed, "Open his eyes, LORD, so that he may see." Then the LORD opened the servant's eyes, and he looked and saw the hills full of horses and chariots of fire all around Elisha. (6:15–17)

Angel armies were surrounding the enemies of God! Struck blind, Elisha's attackers fell into confusion. The prophet led them away, restored their sight by the power of God, and spared their lives. Absolutely astonishing!

I wonder what would happen if God opened our

eyes this way? Like Billy Graham, I believe those of us in a "valley . . . full of foes [would] see the holy angels of God arrayed for battle on [our] behalf." I thank God that we don't have to fight life's battles on our own. God's heavenly host protect and defend us. And like angels, we can fight on behalf of those around us. We do this most powerfully on our knees in prayer. When we intercede for others, we enter the war for goodness, truth, and beauty. Are you ready to do battle for those you love? You can live like an angel by armoring up in prayer!

Be an Angel

For whom can you do battle today? Take a moment to write a prayer for the person God brings to mind. Here's my prayer for you: *Almighty and loving Father, thank You for the precious person reading this book. Whatever challenges today brings, I pray that You'd guide, protect, and defend them. Thank You, Lord, for never leaving us. In Jesus' name, amen.* Now it's your turn to pray for someone else. Feel free to use my words as a guide; you can also speak openly with your Father in heaven.

11

Never Let It Stop You

Courage doesn't mean you don't get afraid. Courage means you don't let fear stop you from trying.
BETHANY HAMILTON, *Be Unstoppable*

If anyone knows about courage, it's Bethany Hamilton. While Hamilton was surfing as a young teen, a tiger shark severed her arm. Undeterred by fear and strengthened by her deep faith in God, she returned to surfing and continues to amaze the world, big-wave surfing with one arm and parenting three boys. Hamilton doesn't let fear stop her. She's a marvelous woman, and I thank God for her example.

I hope you never need the courage to encounter a tiger shark, but I pray that both of us would have the courage we need to face down our fears. Thankfully, courage doesn't always have to be dramatic. Courage can be a quiet and unassuming choice as well. I once thought courage meant the absence of fear. I believed courage should *feel* certain and, well, brave. I had no idea that courage has very little to do with how I'm feeling; it has a lot more to do with what I'm *choosing*.

My hometown of Derry City is a beautiful place in northwest Ireland. I went through quite enough shock moving to England at age eighteen to study art and then theater, but nothing could have adequately prepared me for my transition to New York City. The Big Apple is, hands down, one of the most exhilarating and terrifying places to live.

I felt afraid to move there. I didn't know if I'd "make it." I worried that I might fail. That's when I began a habit that's helped me face fear and embrace courage. When I feel less than courageous about a decision or possibility, I imagine the worst-case scenario. *I could move to New York and get no jobs,* I thought. *I might not make any friends. It may be a huge, expensive mistake.* I couldn't tell myself that these fears were unfounded. They might come true. So I devised a solution to my worst-case scenario: No matter what, I would keep the cost of a return ticket to Ireland in my bank account. If everything else fell apart, I could afford to get home. Making this simple decision gave me courage.

It wasn't always easy to stick with my conviction. There were times I really wanted to spend that money on something else. I refused to do it, though, because courage is often wiser than it is fearless. I've come to discover that wise planning instills courage and banishes fear.

In the biblical accounts of angels visiting Earth, the words "Do not fear" come up a lot. Angels often gave people specific directions from God as well. To Joseph: *Do not divorce Mary; I have asked her to bear My Son, Jesus* (see Matthew 1:18–25). To Paul: *You must stand trial before Caesar* (see Acts 27:23–24). To the shepherds: *Go and find Jesus, the Savior of the world* (see Luke 2:9–15).

Angels dispelled fear and gave wise direction. That combination leads to the kind of courage that can't be taken away, because it comes from God. Will you receive His courage, dear one?

Be an Angel

This may feel very counterintuitive, as most of us are accustomed to avoiding our fears, but deliberately look with God at what worries you. Ask the Holy Spirit to reveal one place where fear is holding you back. Invite Him to show you a wise next step (perhaps a solution to your worst-case scenario). Thank Him for His wisdom. Like an angel might, speak God's words to your own soul: "Do not fear." Breathe this in as often as needed.

12

Don't Be Afraid

O death, where is your victory? O death,
where is your sting?

1 CORINTHIANS 15:55 (NLT)

*D*uring the years we starred on *Touched by an
Angel,* my castmates and I received a good deal
of attention while in public. I loved interacting in person with viewers who welcomed us into their homes
every weekend via television. After all, people invited
us into their sacred spaces—their living rooms and
bedrooms—and into their hearts. It was a privilege to
hear how the show blessed them.

Every now and then, I'd have an odd conversation
with a fan, but if I got the occasional funny look or
quirky comment, it was nothing compared with what
my co-star John Dye experienced. John played Andrew,
the angel of death, and people reacted to his presence
in some hilarious ways. I'd board a flight with John and
hear someone who recognized him exclaim, "I hope
you're not here on a professional assignment!"

In his inimitable way, John would cock his head and

smile wryly, shrugging his shoulders ever so slightly. Everyone would laugh, and any tension would evaporate in the warmth of John's spirit. He just had a way with people.

Tall and handsome, tenderhearted and accessible, John Dye made an impact far beyond the small screen. His gentle yet strong presence as an actor helped people facing death in real life. A man of deep faith, John knew that some viewers might feel afraid or unsure about their future; by God's grace, he could talk to them and help ease their fears. John took this role seriously and blessed people powerfully.

To my daughter, Reilly, he was Uncle Johnny, and she was his "little lamb." We were a tight-knit bunch on set. Long hours and late Friday nights made us a family. We shared life and faced death together.

Eight years after *Touched by an Angel*'s final episode aired, I received a phone call about John's untimely passing. His death pierced my heart. I flew with *Touched by an Angel*'s showrunner, Martha Williamson, to Mississippi for his memorial service. We traded our memories of John, including the way he and I would get the giggles and force the entire team to "take ten" because of our irrepressible laughter. He could bring the most heart-wrenching scene to life, then crack us up the next second.

Every so often, Mark and I will come across an episode of *Touched by an Angel* on TV. It's great to see John's face, if only on the small screen. I miss my friend. Indeed, I miss both my friends John and Della. I marvel at how beautifully they brought their characters to life. Yet I also see God at work in the show. The truth is, *God* starred in each episode; it was never about me or Della or John. I feel so incredibly grateful that God used any of us to help change the way even one viewer saw life, death, and the journey in between.

Death is only a passing into the next life. It doesn't have the final word! The grave doesn't get the victory; Jesus assured that with His resurrection. I have no doubt that when John Dye went home to Jesus, God sent someone precious—someone as special as John's angel-of-death character, Andrew—to help Uncle Johnny make it all the way home. I can't wait to hear the story when I see my friend again.

Be an Angel

What is your current attitude toward death? What did you think when you read the words of 1 Corinthians 15:55, the Bible verse that opened this chapter? Does it comfort you to know that Jesus' sacrifice on the cross means that death has lost its sting for all eternity? How does the thought of eternal rest sound to you? Take some time to think about these things with God by your side.

13

Go With

Be strong and courageous. Do not be afraid
or terrified because of them, for the LORD
your God goes with you; he will never leave
you nor forsake you.

DEUTERONOMY 31:6

I recently posted this verse to my social media
story one morning just after dawn. With the rest
of the world, I had been watching a terrible international conflict evolve thousands of miles away. Feelings
of fear and hopelessness threatened; I knew that I
needed to press into the hope of God's Word and the
peace of His presence. So I meditated on this heavenly
assurance from Deuteronomy and shared it as a first-
light promise with everyone in my circle.

God's present "withness" changes everything. It up-
lifts and strengthens us. On the other hand, when we
feel alone or afraid, we're less than our best selves. Fear
shortens our emotional fuses. Worry suppresses creativ-
ity and productivity. Anxiety robs us of joy and hope.
The truth that God never leaves nor forsakes us does

the exact opposite: It extends our emotional bandwidth, encourages vision, and fans the flame of confidence. When we *go with God* throughout our day, we greet what comes our way with strength and courage.

Some years ago, doctors diagnosed our son Cameron with a brain tumor. Our entire world seemed upside down as we met with neurosurgeons and oncologists. A teenager at the time, our son should have been in the prime of his life! Although his cancer caught us completely by surprise, I am very grateful that it did not catch *God* by surprise.

God carried our family through exhausting days at the hospital, through months of recovery, through wondering if Cameron would ever walk again, and through endless questions, prayers, and tears. Mark and I clung to Deuteronomy 31:6 during this time. Knowing that God would not leave us was the life-giving, hopeful, and empowering truth we needed. Praise God, Cameron made a miraculous recovery.

Sometimes that seems like quite a long time ago; during other moments, I might reel with the memory. Times and seasons change, but our need for God with us never does. These days, I often find the loneliness of leadership upon me. Directing a production team and getting a project off the ground means making difficult decisions. I deliberately go with God through my days by involving Him in every decision. Whether the issue is big or small, whether my family is facing down giants or I'm navigating everyday work, I pray, listen, and walk in step with His Spirit. I go with God because with Him is courage and strength, hope and peace. God goes before and behind me, just as He always has for His people.

In the book of Exodus, God proclaimed, "See, I am sending an angel ahead of you to guard you along the way and to bring you to the place I have prepared" (23:20). I've experienced this same sense of His presence and protection as He brings me to every place He has prepared. I haven't always liked where the path leads, at least not immediately. No one wants their son to become ill! I can affirm, however, that even the dark places of my journey have led me to something good when I've gone with God. I pray He helps you see the same, dear friend.

Be an Angel

Loneliness isn't simply a feeling to endure; it can also reveal something about us. When do you feel most alone? How does that help you better understand yourself? Now think about what God's withness looks like for you. How might you go with God in your lonely moments?

Forgiveness

14

Ask

There was somewhere, deep inside my heart, that I thought . . . maybe you had done something to get here. I'm sorry. Please forgive me.
MONICA, *Touched by an Angel*

It has been nearly two decades since *Touched by an Angel* filmed its final season. All these years later, my memory doesn't keep every detail neatly organized, but some episodes stand apart, crystal clear in my mind. "There But for the Grace of God" is one of those.

In this story, God sends my angel character, Monica, to help restore dignity and hope to Pete, who lost his wife, livelihood, and self-worth. In so doing, Monica must confront her own assumptions about homelessness and those experiencing it. God strips Monica of her angelic powers for a time so she can truly understand what it's like to live on the streets, harshly judged and mercilessly cast off by society.

Touched by an Angel always included an "angel revelation" scene, the moment when God's messengers

dropped their undercover human identities and un-
veiled God's purpose for those they were serving. It
was the heart of every episode, and filming it always
felt powerful and significant. In "There But for the
Grace of God," this scene takes place on a dirty street
in the dead of night.

Exhausted and hopeless, Pete faces the very present
danger of freezing to death. He was ejected from a shel-
ter after someone stole the backpack containing the
only thing that still mattered to him: the urn with his
wife's ashes. Monica finds Pete, confesses that she's
judged him, and asks if he will forgive her. Wrongly
believing he had done something to land himself on
the streets had kept Monica from serving Pete as God
intended. In humility and love, she washes Pete's dirty
and wounded feet. This humble act of compassion re-
stores Monica's powers and Pete's dignity. With Monica
by Pete's side, God enables Pete to tenderly say goodbye
to his wife and move forward with hope.

Filming this episode changed me. I never thought of
myself as a person with assumptions or prejudices. But
God allowed me to see, just like Monica does, that
"somewhere, deep inside my heart," there were places
Love Himself needed to heal and transform.

To be set free from the poison of her presumptions,
Monica has to ask for Pete's forgiveness. I realized *I*
need forgiveness too. In fact, we all need forgiveness,

not simply for the hurtful things we've done but also for the hurtful things we've believed and thought. It's easy to miss this complex dynamic of the human condition since we more readily see the wrongs done to us than we do our own mistakes.

Dear friend, as you read these words, did you feel God lovingly pressing on any assumptions or beliefs you have about someone? Forgiveness alone sets you free; asking for forgiveness enables you to live with compassion rather than contempt. In my opinion, trading presumption for peace sounds like a pretty good deal. What do you think?

Be an Angel

God sends my angel character, Monica, to learn about her heart from those experiencing homelessness. If you were an angel for a day, where might God send you? Are there beliefs or judgments that may be involved in your answer? If so, consider asking God's forgiveness for anything that is presently blocking His love for others. The freedom of forgiveness is yours for the taking.

15

Follow . . . to the Very End

Jesus said, "Father, forgive them, for they
do not know what they are doing."

LUKE 23:34

I had no idea.

I had never filmed a crucifixion scene before.

I imagined that watching a reenactment of Jesus'
death would be difficult, but none of us—cast or
crew—realized how physically and emotionally de-
manding it would be. The brutality and horror of crucifixion came through powerfully.

After Mark and I began developing *The Bible* miniseries, we spent weeks casting each critical role. Find-
ing actors to play two of the most important characters
proved quite difficult. God miraculously connected us
with Diogo Morgado, who took on the role of Jesus.
This was after I sent an email to prayer warriors with
the subject line "Looking for Jesus." Still, we had not
found an actress to play Christ's mother, Mary, as
an adult. After our many frustrating hours scrolling
through résumés and headshots, my husband said with

perfect frankness, "I don't know why you're missing the obvious. You need to take this role yourself." I was shocked but agreed to pray about it. That night, God filled me with a knowing peace that this was *His* invitation.

Now here I was, garbed as Jesus' mother and standing at the foot of a cross, watching Diogo, whom I'd grown to love like a son, act out the crucifixion of Christ. The flogging, the blood, the hatred of the mob—none of it was literally real, but every bit of it was more real than ever.

Never had the incomprehensibility of Jesus' final words struck me so forcefully. In the moment of His torturous execution, Jesus forgave. Because I was playing Mary, I had to imagine what it might have felt like for this mother to hear her son say, "Father, forgive them, for they do not know what they are doing." The reality hit me: I'm not sure I could have forgiven while watching my son savagely executed. But if Jesus chose to forgive, how can I harbor unforgiveness toward someone?

Most people acknowledge that they'd like to forgive . . . at least eventually. Cognitively speaking, we know that holding on to our wounds doesn't actually help us. Despite this, we usually need time to forgive. Jesus forgave instantaneously, but it sometimes takes us a while to lay our burdens down.

True, I can't forgive *like* Jesus, but I can forgive *because of* Jesus. I can forgive because He made it possible. All of us can forgive because He first forgave freely, lovingly, completely.

Just before His death, Jesus prayed in a lonely garden called Gethsemane. The Bible tells us that an angel ministered to Him there, comforting and strengthening Him (see Luke 22:43). God sent an angel to help Jesus face what lay ahead, including the need to radically forgive. If there's something you've been unable to forgive, I invite you to ask for the same care God provided His Son. He will strengthen and comfort you as you follow in Jesus' footsteps. Today is the day, dear one, to follow to the very end.

Be an Angel

Is there someone you know who is currently suffering from their own resentment and bitterness? How might you be like an angel who comforts and strengthens them as they start to forgive?

16

Be Set Free

When we forgive, we set a prisoner free and
discover that the prisoner we set free is us.

LEWIS B. SMEDES, *The Art of Forgiving*

*W*here should we put the crosses, Ms. Downey?"
It was a simple question, but it caught me
off guard. I realized in the split second before I responded that the team looked to me as the expert.

Gulp. Pray. Breathe. Trust God to lead.

"Let's set up over here," I answered.

An early-spring chill clung to the rocky terrain of
Matera, Italy. As I looked back at the cityscape, cut into
limestone outcroppings, the twenty-first century and
the first blurred together. Amid these ancient stones,
enemies of Rome were once barbarously executed.

We had been on location, filming *Ben-Hur* for some
time, but it was this day that we'd begin filming the
crucifixion of Jesus. Because I was one of the movie's
executive producers and, by this point, had overseen
two other cinematic portrayals of Christ's death, everyone expected me to know what to do and how to do

it. I quickly recognized that it never gets easier to trace Jesus' footsteps to the cross.

Mark and I had made an early decision to tie Jesus to Judah Ben-Hur's story in a more definitive way than the original film from 1959 had. We shot one scene of Jesus carrying, through a busy marketplace, the heavy crossbeam on which He'd die. Under its weight, depleted from blood loss and extreme exhaustion, driven by a merciless praetorian guard, Jesus collapses. Judah Ben-Hur quickly draws water to relieve Christ's suffering but receives a blow from a Roman soldier's sharp whip in return.

Filled with rage, Judah picks up a rock. All the hatred stored in his heart, all the wrongs done to him, and the betrayal of his childhood friend and adopted brother erupt in an unquenchable longing for vengeance. Before he can turn to cast the stone, however, Jesus clasps His own hand over Judah's.

"My life—I give it of My own free will," Christ whispers.

The crowd swells, the soldiers force Jesus on to Golgotha, and Judah fades into the masses standing near Christ's cross. His hand closes more tightly around the rock as he watches Jesus, an innocent man, die. With His last breaths, Jesus prays, "Father, forgive them, for they know not what they do." Christ surrenders His spirit and dies.

Slowly, unconsciously, Judah Ben-Hur releases his clenched fist. The rock falls, and the journey of forgiveness begins. To that point, hatred and unforgiveness had kept Judah in bondage. At the cross, in opening his hand to forgive, Judah discovers he can be free. Whether his enemies live or die, whether they acknowledge their wrongs or not, he can move forward in freedom. Forgiveness is the path for Judah; it is also the path for us.

Forgiveness doesn't excuse or erase the wrongs done to us. It doesn't let the "other guy" off the hook. It simply sets us free from the bitterness that corrodes our souls. Instead of holding on to the burning coal we intend to hurl at whoever wounded us, we open our hands. Sure, we can keep getting burned by unforgiveness, but we don't have to. We can be set free instead.

Be an Angel

Imagine God sent an angel to give you a choice between holding on to and letting go of wrongs done to you. What would you choose? What *will* you choose? Take a moment to breathe in the presence of Christ. Are there any rocks you're clutching tightly? Might today be the day to open your hand?

17

Forgive

The remedy for life's broken pieces is not classes,
workshops, or books. Don't try to heal
the broken pieces. Just forgive.

Iyanla Vanzant

have two beloved friends who have endured terrible divorces. Their husbands behaved abominably. One girlfriend has courageously moved past her pain into a new life. The other remains stuck, angry, and bitter. The difference between these women? Pure and simple: forgiveness.

Whether we're ruled by or set free from our deepest wounds comes down to a myriad of choices, some great and some small. I've gone through seasons when forgiveness came readily and other times when it welled up slowly. Forgiveness isn't a one-size-fits-all proposition.

Wouldn't it be nice if forgiveness followed a formula? Do X, think Y, pray Z, and—voilà!—you're free of resentment. That's not how forgiveness works, though. We can spin our wheels on classes, workshops, and books, trying to heal the broken parts of our lives. But I can affirm, as Psalm 18:20 does, that "GOD made my life complete when I placed all the pieces before him" (MSG, emphasis added). Only God's forgiveness makes healing possible.

To say "Just forgive" doesn't mean forgiveness is easy. Forgiveness is a costly journey—emotionally, spiritually, sometimes even physically. By quoting the directive to just forgive, I simply mean to encourage you not to get distracted by a million self-help options. Pursue forgiveness because it alone leads to complete healing.

Too often we're held back by thoughts like *He doesn't deserve forgiveness!* or *Forgiving her is like saying what she did wasn't that bad; well, it* was *that bad.* Yes, often it was. And the truth is, no one deserves forgiveness. Forgiveness flows only from grace, which means it's given freely, not based on merit.

Instead of allowing thoughts like *How dare he?* and *I'll never forgive her* to live rent-free in our minds and hearts, let's imagine what else that mental and emotional space might hold if we let go. If resentment robs the present moment of joy and the future of freedom— and it *does* rob us in this way—why keep hanging on?

Perhaps we just don't know where to start. It can feel so daunting to think about forgiving the people who wounded us. Are we supposed to forgive like a magic trick? Abracadabra, and all the pain is gone?

Thankfully, no. We aren't asked to forgive like that. Indeed, we *can't* forgive like that. God alone can forgive instantly, wholeheartedly, with no residual pain. Instead, we are invited to start with the smallest step, a step of intentionality: "I want to lay this down. Jesus, I need Your help to forgive."

Beginning with this intention moves us one thought nearer to God. Staying in close touch with Him through prayer is central to continuing this process. The Holy Spirit guides us on the path of freedom and forgiveness one small step, one thought, one choice, and one action at a time.

We don't have to hold on to the hurts people have done to us; we do have a choice. Dear one, why not bring your broken parts to God today? Place them before the One who loves you, the One who died to make forgiveness possible. Will you allow Him to make the puzzle of your life complete? He knows how to fit every fragmented piece together.

Be an Angel

How do you feel about starting with an intention to forgive today? Perhaps it's time to say, "I want to be able to lay this down. I don't know how, but I want to forgive."

Hope

18

Look Forward to It

A story is being told, and the best is yet to come!
ROMA DOWNEY

Some years ago, Mark and I were enjoying a day of Christmas shopping together. At some point, we bought a lovely plaque as a gift to each other. It read, "Grow old with me. The best is yet to be."

Robert Browning's sentiment resonated with us deeply, expressing the gifts of companionship, partnership, and love that God has given. Those words also reminded us of how we want to live: with anticipation and eagerness.

Mark and I deliberately choose to greet the future with openness and joy. We're both increasingly aware of the passage of time and how we change as a result. We work long, hard hours and look forward to spending more time with our children or in nature or both! We choose to believe that "the best is yet to be," and that changes how we navigate good and bad days now.

Some of my beloved girlfriends view the passing of time with deep sadness; they primarily forecast a series of losses as the years fly by. While this is understandable on one level, it seems to hurt, not help, my friends. Life can be difficult, and it may not always feel easy to believe, but trusting that "the best is yet to be" changes us for the better. Holding hope close to our hearts becomes a beautiful and empowering way to regard the future.

If you've already embraced this perspective, wonderful! Keep on, dear one. If this idea is new for you, today is a wonderful day to start reframing. Bring to mind one thing that you can anticipate with joy. Is it an upcoming birthday you can make extra special for someone you love? Is it a walk on your favorite trail or beach, or a bite into a summer peach or crisp fall apple? The Bible tells us that God is the giver of all good gifts (see James 1:17). Think about it: He's given us so many people and things to enjoy.

Another small way you can begin the process of reframing is by considering who helps you feel brighter and more hopeful about the days to come. Mark certainly does this for me, as do my beloved daughter and my amazing stepsons. Choose to spend time with those who embrace a perspective that "the best is yet to be."

Finally, remember what God's angelic messenger told the shepherds in the book of Luke: "I bring you good tidings of great joy" (2:10, NKJV). Like angels, we can be messengers of hope and joy. We can do this in our homes, at our workplaces, and even through our online posts. We can be like angels spreading light, reminding people of God's love. He promises that all of us can join Him in heaven for an eternity with no pain or sorrow if we receive the sacrifice of His Son, Jesus, for our sin. This means that the best *really, truly* is yet to come. Let's celebrate that today!

Be an Angel

All too often, social media overflows with bad news of a bleak future. Why not bring tidings of joy instead? You could post Robert Browning's words "The best is yet to be" and invite your friends to comment with one thing they're looking forward to. You'll be spreading hope as you do.

19

Dream Again

You are never too old to set another goal
or to dream a new dream.

LES BROWN, *Live Your Dreams*

hat does the word *old* bring to mind? How does the passing of time make you feel? How do change, transitions, goals, and dreams affect you?

God has blessed me with a very full life. I've lived in His love, following His direction, for decades now. There are many experiences—joyful and painful—behind me. Change and transition have kept me company on the journey, and they haven't always been the most comfortable companions.

After almost a decade on *Touched by an Angel,* I went through a season of personal and professional transition. The intensity of twelve-hour (or more) workdays and all the accompanying marketing and publicity gave way to the quiet of a post-show life that was both lovely (I needed the rest!) *and* challenging (Who am I without my work?).

A similar season of transition occurred for Mark and

me when we became empty nesters. The beautiful busyness of raising three children turned into the celebration of their adult lives and accomplishments. Our home felt so different, though. We lamented with friends over the simultaneously joyous and agonizing change from family dinners and school productions to solitary evenings.

During both seasons of change, God impressed on my heart the need to dream again, to set goals that He could help me fulfill. Jesus reaffirmed that I was not too old to be used by Him, nor would I ever be.

As time passes, we face the temptation to settle in. We may feel more comfortable saying yes to limits and restrictions than to dreams and goals. They feel risky (*What if I fail?*). Self-doubt and fear often come with transition, change, and aging, but they need not define us. In my seasons of transition, I pressed into discovering who God made me to be: not limited by a TV show or even by the best of roles, motherhood.

God placed a dream on my heart to start a production company. I wanted to share stories of life and love, hope and joy. I wanted to bring His light to the entertainment industry. But to do so, I had to resolutely resist self-doubting and fearful thoughts. I needed to trust God to fulfill His dream in me. And He has!

Once upon a time, all of us had dreams and goals. What stops us from dreaming as time passes? Usually, it's fear that paralyzes us. When we invite God to conquer our fear, though, we receive exhilarating and empowering energy to dream again, to set goals, to live bold and free.

In Luke 1:5–25, we read the remarkable story of a couple, Elizabeth and Zechariah, who "were both very old" (verse 7). How's that for a blunt description? Miraculously, an angel of God brought good news to Zechariah: "Your wife Elizabeth will bear you a son, and you are to call him John. He will be a joy and delight to you, and many will rejoice because of his birth, for he will be great in the sight of the Lord" (verses 13–15). We know Elizabeth and Zechariah's son by the title history gave him (John the Baptist) and by his role: forerunner to and minister alongside Jesus. The world thought of John's parents as past their prime; God saw things differently. No one is ever too old to be used by God for something great. It's time to dream again with Him, dear one.

Be an Angel

If you knew you couldn't fail, what would you do? Let your imag-
ination run wild. Write down any and every thought, no matter
how crazy it seems. God has given you this time and space to
dream. Pray over your list, asking Him to highlight one dream;
then ask Him to help you formulate a goal attached to it. Let's
dream together.

20

Lean into Longing

Oh, Danny boy, the pipes, the pipes are calling. . . .
The summer's gone, and all the roses falling. . . .
It's you must go and I must bide.
"Danny Boy," traditional Irish ballad, lyrics
attributed to Frederic Weatherly

The lockdowns of the Covid-19 pandemic left me quite homesick. I didn't return to Ireland for almost three years while the virus churned, leaving the world in various states of chaos and confusion. I'd been so used to flying home regularly; when that simply wasn't possible, I felt heartsick.

I always looked forward to my visits home; sometimes merely stepping off the plane onto Irish soil gave me a sense of peace and comfort. Other times the homesickness intensified. Why? How?

Then I learned a Welsh word for this experience: *hiraeth*. It's a mixture of yearning and nostalgia, an earnest desire for what has been lost. *Hiraeth* describes homesickness tinged with grief and desire. I have known hiraeth for a very long time.

Losing first my mother and then my father while I was still young left me with longings this world couldn't answer. Mom used to sing me to sleep at night, almost always the same song: "You'll Never Walk Alone," from the musical *Carousel*. Dad took a different bedtime approach after my mother died. He'd read poetry to me as I lay under the covers, enraptured by images like those in "The Lake Isle of Innisfree." William Butler Yeats's magnificent poem gave my feelings words: "I hear lake water lapping with low sounds by the shore; . . . I hear it in the deep heart's core."[9]

In my deep heart's core, I yearn for my parents. I'm heartsick for what I've been blessed to have and lose. I hear the water lapping on the shores of my homeland and traditional Irish melodies like "Danny Boy" echoing within.

The poetry of Yeats, poignant folk lyrics, my homesickness—all evoke hiraeth. This Welsh term illuminates my own experience and the universal human condition as well. We all yearn for something; we long for someone. We don't always understand the language of wistful nostalgia our hearts speak, because we ultimately ache for a home where no loss, sickness, or fear can touch us. In short, we long for heaven.

We try to quiet our yearning with busyness, accomplishments, or relationships. Those are marvelous blessings, but we were made for even more. Only faith, hope, and love enable us to make it, through the heartache of life, to our true home with God. Hope anchors me when hiraeth storms rage. What about you, dear one?

I don't know where today finds you. I celebrate if the roses in your life are in full bloom. My heart hurts with you if you're facing a season of deep grief, perhaps after the loss of a loved one or of dreams stolen by circumstances. Our hope is in this: One day Jesus " 'will wipe every tear. . . . There will be no more death' or mourning or crying or pain, for the old order of things has passed away" (Revelation 21:4). Faith enables us to both feel the ache and look forward with hope. And, as Romans 5:5 says, "Hope does not put us to shame, because God's love has been poured out into our hearts through the Holy Spirit, who has been given to us."

I pray today that hope fills you, softening any hiraeth you feel. I pray you might speak hope into the lives of those around you. Like God's angels, let's tell others of the hope found in the Lord.

Be an Angel

Lean into your longing today. What does it tell you? What does your heart ache for? Write a prayer or journal entry, entrusting your desire to God with hope in your heart.

21

Sow Hope

*Judge each day not by the harvest you reap
but by the seeds you plant.*
attributed to WILLIAM ARTHUR WARD

eveloping any creative work requires a great deal of effort. Getting a television series, movie, or book into production can feel like pulling teeth. People often assume it's glamorous to be in "the biz," but what takes us a couple of hours to watch or a few days to read involves months (or even years!) of hard work by massive teams of people.

I recently went through quite a long "planting" season. I sowed the seeds of several projects, and the tending of each consumed my days. There were literal years of no fruit to enjoy or harvest to celebrate. And I'll be honest: There were times of doubt and frustration. Every creative endeavor comes with risk; I didn't know how things would turn out. But I pressed on, trusting that beauty would bloom. I sowed with intention and planted with hope. I worked with diligence and prayed with passion.

And then it happened in the most unexpected way. I turned on my computer and checked my email. Virtual silence. No urgent requests, no budgets to approve, no problems to solve, no pages to edit. I actually wondered if the internet had failed.

It finally occurred to me that I had moved into a season of harvest. The hard work had started to pay off; the heavy lifting was done. What joy! Sowing and waiting had been difficult, but the rewards were rich. If I had judged each previous day by its harvest, I could have easily become discouraged.

We may understand the rhythm of planting and produce when it comes to the natural world. We know a bulb doesn't become a tulip overnight, and it takes time for a sapling to grow into a thirty-foot tree! But we're a bit impatient with growth in relationships, maturity, or mission. We want results tomorrow or—better yet—today! We want instant feedback: a text, a comment, a like, or a repost. But expecting a constant harvest is quite exhausting.

As parents, we plant seeds in our children that may take a lifetime to bloom. We patiently engage in one more conversation, offering a single piece of counsel or a truckload of prayers. And then we must wait. Raising a child is not an overnight process.

In our work, we may pour hours and hours into a project. Risk may be necessary; we don't have any guarantees. But we sow with intention and plant with hope. Sometimes the harvest is plentiful, and sometimes we face famine. No matter the season, what we choose to focus on changes everything.

So, dear one, how will you look at this day, this month, this year? Are you in a sowing or a reaping season? Though we cannot control the seasons of our lives or the results of our planting and reaping, we do have control over our attitudes. Let's cultivate a perspective that embraces what each season brings.

Be an Angel

One way to live like God's angelic messengers is to plant seeds of love and hope in the lives of others. Think of a person who's been working hard for some time. Why not send that person a message or mail a card, letting them know that you see their diligence and look forward to the harvest that will come from all their effort?

Faith

22

Don't Keep This Secret

My secret is simple: I pray.
attributed to MOTHER TERESA

ine times out of ten, keeping a secret is best. When people tell us something confidential, we honor them by holding their trust. Some secrets, however, shouldn't be kept. And this secret—I'm talking about the power of prayer—is one I'm never going to keep.

I call it a secret because I'm often asked, "How can you stay so calm, Roma? What's your secret?" This isn't to say that I'm never fazed by hard things; I'm just not prone to massive reactions. People know about the pain in my past: the loss of my parents, relationship heartache, our son's brain tumor. They wonder how I remain peaceful and balanced.

It's simple: I pray.

And because the power of prayer rests in the One hearing my prayers, not in my saying them, I know the calm is not about me. It is and always has been about

God.[10] The relationship I enjoy with Him in prayer is the primary reason I am who I am.

I feel quite fortunate to have been taught about prayer early in life. My father loved God and prayed often. Dad raised me Catholic, and I memorized prayers at church. He also told me that prayer is speaking to God from the heart, and that meant I could pray anywhere, anytime.

I have. And I do.

I often wonder why we overcomplicate the life of faith. We think we must be in a certain building or even in a certain mood to talk with God. Prayer doesn't have to be formal or static, though. We can speak to God from our hearts. Isn't that glorious? If there's a secret to my steadiness and centeredness, it's God's presence in my anywhere, anytime prayers.

I've made it my habit to awaken the morning with prayers of wonder and gratitude. Starting my day this way changes everything. I also pray throughout the day. When I'm happy, I thank God. When I'm anxious, I seek His help. When colleagues are arguing in front of me, I pray for them, asking God to bring peace and resolution. When I'm confused, I turn to Him. When I'm angry, I confess my need for Him. Do you see where I'm going with this? No matter what's happening, I pray.

This is especially helpful when people I love are suffering. I can't always do something tangible to help, let alone "fix things." Our son Cameron's brain tumor brought this truth into sharp focus. I could pray and pray and pray some more; I could do little else. But guess what? Prayer was enough. It *is* enough.

Because God's angelic host aren't affected by sin like we are, they have a special kind of unbroken fellowship with Him. I believe we can live more like angels here on Earth by talking with God all through the day, no matter what we're facing. Indeed, I don't just think we can do this; I believe this is what we were made for. Let's not settle for anything less!

Be an Angel

Receive the gift of anywhere, anytime prayer for yourself today. Enjoy intimacy with the Lover of your soul. Why not share the secret of prayer with someone else too? You can be like an angel, demonstrating the special closeness with God available in prayer.

23

Be Still and Know

*When it feels as if you're walking alone, searching for
light in darkness, be still, and know that I am God.*
my reflection on PSALM 46:10

Psalm 46:10 is one of my favorite scriptures. For
me, these words are applicable anytime, anywhere. No matter how alone I feel or how dark my
circumstances seem, I can always enter the stillness of
God's presence. There I find light because He is the
Light of the World. There I find peace because Jesus is
the Prince of Peace. There I find hope, for He is the
Hope that anchors me.

"Be still, and know that I am God" is a command as
well as an invitation. It's an imperative: "Stop now, dear
friend, before it is too late!" It's also an invitation: "In
the stillness you will know Me; this is what your heart
truly needs."

Our online world is busier and noisier than ever. We
could easily scroll, post, like, comment, or subscribe all
day, every day. We could curate our images or feeds
endlessly. But this isn't what we were made for. We

were made for relationship, both with the One who formed us and with others. We were made for beauty, reflective of our glorious Creator. It's so essential in our frenetic world to step aside and *be* with God in stillness.

I do this by deliberately creating space in my day. Instead of rushing between meetings, and activities, or even online perusing, I keep guard over times of transition. Between appointments and tasks, I take cleansing breaths, turn my attention to God, and am renewed by Him.

Sometimes I do this in prayer, other times through a verse from God's Word. Often I use the shift between activities to experience His presence in nature. I go outside and look for flowers that just bloomed, listen for birds singing, or feel the warm breeze or the crisp bite in the air. I return to simply *being,* not merely *doing* one more thing. God meets me in those moments, and I will not give them up.

Psalm 46 is an extremely rich chapter of Scripture. Its depth ranges from the wars men wage, to the humility we feel when we witness natural phenomena, to how God protects His people. The waters run deep in this psalm, yet there is also beautiful simplicity in verse 10: "Be still, and know that I am God." We don't have to overcomplicate drawing near to Him; we can be close to Him every single day.

In the Bible, angels repeatedly praised God for who

He is. The heavenly host know Him and speak of Him with joyful celebration: " 'Holy, holy, holy is the Lord God Almighty,' who was, and is, and is to come" (Revelation 4:8). When we are still and know that He is God, we grow in our ability to know Him and respond to Him. We learn, in the stillness, to thank and exalt Him for who He is, in a way similar to the angels who eternally proclaim His glory.

Beloved one, don't miss the joy of unplugging from the "musts" and "have-tos" so you can be still and know that He is God.

Be an Angel

Take a moment to get up and step outside. What part of God's creation can you delight in? Can you see a tree? What is the wind saying? Be still for a moment. Breathe in the presence of the One closer to you than your very breath, and listen for His "still small voice" (1 Kings 19:12, NKJV).

24

Embrace the Journey

We live by faith, not by sight.

2 CORINTHIANS 5:7

Faith is a journey.

Scratch that. Faith is *the* journey of the human heart. We live in a world that constantly demands faith. The question isn't whether you and I have faith but rather in what or whom we place our faith.

I've decided to place my faith in God. All my eggs are in His basket. I'm not spreading my faith around, hoping to ensure a positive outcome. I've chosen to live by faith (in Him), not by sight (in my own strength).

That's not always easy, is it? If you're anything like me, certainty and sight feel a lot safer. I'm more comfortable when I can see several steps ahead. Most of us like to think we can predict an outcome. We like to feel in control. The need for certainty feels very real and pressing. But the truth is, we have very little control in life. I learned this early in my childhood, when my beloved mother died. At the same time, I also learned that faith could settle my heart in a way that sight could not.

Growing up, I went to a Catholic school, and one of my teachers shared that even our troubles can be pathways to closeness with God. I felt the truth of that. I could see it reflected in my own life. This lesson landed squarely on my heart probably because, especially in the years just after Mom went to be with God, I needed Jesus to show up so very much. Through that same lesson at school, I also learned that trying to manage things on my own—my pride—separated me from God. I didn't want that, so I chose faith rather than sight. I've been making the same decision ever since.

Working with various guest stars on *Touched by an Angel* further affirmed the importance of walking by faith. Because we had guest appearances on every episode, Della and I enjoyed weekly conversations with a wide variety of people. As they told us their stories, sharing their journeys of faith and struggle, I marveled at the miraculous and mysterious ways God worked. A guest actor might book a role on our show and discover that their character's story line mirrored their own. Perhaps they grew up with an alcoholic father or lost a sister in a car accident; filming the episode often brought hope or healing to them. Della and I would sit back in awe and wonder at how God works. We can see His fingerprints everywhere if we look with the eyes of faith.

During my journey of healing after my mother's

passing, God didn't show up for me in a flaming bush; He didn't divide the Irish Sea. He came in the form of a peace I felt in my heart—a peace that transcends understanding (see Philippians 4:6–7). For most of us, God won't show up with trumpets sounding and angels singing in the sky; He comes in the quiet moments that require faith to see.

I don't know where today finds you—whether you are feeling like you can conquer the world or are drowning in sorrow. Dear one, my heart goes out to you. The human journey is intense. First Peter 1:12 reveals that "even angels long to look into these things"—that is, the mysteries of faith, the gospel, and God's redemption of mankind.

Wherever you are today, I pray that you'd open your heart, like an angel, to "look into" faith, to give it your attention. With me, dear one, embrace the journey. Breathe in God's presence, His love, His peace.

Be an Angel

Spend a few moments looking back over the events of your life. In what ways can you trace God's hand? Where are His fingerprints evident? If signs of Him are difficult to see, you can invite Him to open your eyes with greater faith. He will do this because His love is *for you* . . . always.

25

Tell the Story

It's a love story. It's God's love story for us from the moment Adam and Eve fell from grace. . . . From that moment, we have been trying to get home to God and [we have] continually messed up. But God loved us so much that he sent his only son to bring us home.

from my interview with the *Irish Independent*

As a girl in religious studies class, I never imagined myself explaining the Bible to millions of people. But here I was, describing to a journalist God's plan for redemption highlighted in *The Bible* miniseries. I told him that I was excited, eager, and sometimes quite nervous. I wanted to get it right.

I wanted people to understand that God's Word is a love story. It's a story of being lost and found, wandering away and returning home. No matter how often we've messed up, God's love never fails. I wanted people's faith to grow as they watched each episode.

Instead of viewing God's Word as disconnected narratives, Mark and I wanted to reinforce that the Bible is a love story that fits together, Genesis through Revelation. We discussed different ways to communicate this. Some ideas made it to the final cut, while others ended up on the editing-room floor. All of them reflected our passion for this project.

Part of our work involved researching scenes in Jerusalem, on the Via Dolorosa, the Way of Suffering. Tradition holds that Jesus walked this road with His cross. Millions of pilgrims travel this winding path every year, touching stones that Jesus Himself may have passed. In one place, faithful believers have literally worn down the stone by touching and kissing the wall.

"What are the chances Jesus *actually* rested His hand here?" Mark wondered aloud.

I didn't know the answer to that, but I did know this: We can't always *see* faith, but here faith was evident. It was potent. Faith had worn away stone.

Back on set, we shot footage of Diogo, who played Jesus, at this place. We focused on his face and utilized a special camera lens to zoom all the way into his iris. Through editing, his eye slowly morphed into an image of planet Earth. The first words of Genesis rang out: "In the beginning . . ."

From the beginning, God's purpose was redemption; His plan was always love. His love story takes many twists and turns—humans mess things up continually— but God's will cannot be thwarted. He wins His beloved back from sin and death. This is the substance of faith.

Faith doesn't rest in a set of principles. Faith falls on the shoulders of Jesus, the One who made the heavens and earth, the sea and sky, you and me. Faith that carries us all the way home is the great theme of God's love story. Our true home is a place of peace, love, and joy. That is what we universally long for; that is the story the Bible unfolds.

When angels came to Earth, they often corrected human misunderstandings. People kept placing their faith in the wrong things, veering off course from God's love and believing lies. As His messengers, angels always directed people back to His truth. I want to be like an angel by telling God's love story with my life. What about you?

Be an Angel

How have you viewed the Bible? Is it easy or difficult for you to imagine the grand narrative of the Bible as a love story? Like an angel might, how can you help tell the story of God's love with your life?

Gratitude

26

Start the Day

Watch, now, how I start the day in happiness, in kindness.

MARY OLIVER, "Why I Wake Early"

I wasn't always a morning person. In my home country, Ireland, dawn often arrived wet and cold. When one wants to burrow under a down comforter against the damp chill outside, jumping out of bed to greet the day isn't the most natural reaction. Then I moved to a warmer climate, and my energies shifted. I started getting up with the birds and marveling at the sunrise.

If you ever look at my social media, you'll notice how many videos and pictures of sunrises I post. I find myself regularly in awe of dawn's beauty. And I love inviting others to participate in wonder with me.

One of the things I adore about a sunrise is the certainty of it. No matter what happened yesterday or how long the night felt, the sun always rises again. This reassures me powerfully. Even if it's a cold day, sunlight brings warmth with it. Sometimes the gentle glow of dawn gets me through the entire day.

Perhaps that's why Mary Oliver's poem "Why I Wake Early" resonates with me deeply. She likens the sun to a great preacher, and I agree. In the rising sun, we can see a visual promise of resurrection every single morning. *Thank You, God. Thank You.* The sun holds us all in its great hands, Oliver continues. *Yes and amen! Thank You, Light of the World, for holding us close.*

If you're not a morning person and feel worried that the "Be an Angel" challenge at the end of this entry includes getting up at dawn for the rest of your life, fear not! My encouragement isn't about what time you rise but about how you choose to start the day.

How you and I begin something is important, isn't it? It sets the tone for the rest of the experience or activity. How we start each day is significant too. That's why I choose to "start the day in happiness, in kindness." Instead of focusing on my to-do list, I begin the day with gratitude: *Thank You, God, for this new day.*

Rather than grumbling about what didn't get done yesterday, which could easily turn me into a grouch, I start the day by spending time with God in prayer and meditation. I greet my husband with love and bring him a cup of tea first thing; this sets the tempo for our interactions all day. I even treat my furry family, my beloved dogs, with kindness because they are gifts from God, and I do not take them for granted.

The book of Job says that the angels were there as God created the earth (see 38:4–7). That means they would have seen the very first sunrise. Wow! I can only imagine how stunning that must have been. Although we didn't have that particular privilege, we do have great joy available to us every new day. Why don't we start the day in kindness and gratitude together?

Be an Angel

Tomorrow morning is an invitation to joy. As you go through the rest of this day, remind yourself that tomorrow you will begin the day with a grateful heart, treating others with kindness. Try this for a few days running and see what else changes as a result.

27

Pay Attention

Gratitude arises from paying attention, from
being awake in the presence of everything.
DAVID WHYTE, *Consolations*

*H*umans can't thrive while panting. Shallow
breaths work for short spells—when you're
about to miss a flight and have to sprint to the gate, for
instance—but, really, we're designed to need deep,
cleansing breaths to renew the oxygen in our cells. Few
of us realize that we're racing through life, forcing our
lungs into a pattern of shallow breathing. But when we
begin to breathe deeply, we awaken more fully.

During my training at Drama Studio London, I
learned to attend to each breath I took. To project my
voice in a theater without amplification, I needed to
engage my diaphragm. I knew this would be important
professionally, but I had no idea at the time how helpful
this would be for me personally. Clearing my body and
mind with deep, purposeful breaths keeps me awake to
the present, grateful for what's before me.

I initially made this connection when I learned about

meditation. I didn't quite understand the difference between prayer and meditation when I began. I knew
how to pray from the time I was very young, but I
didn't have much training in meditating on the name of
Jesus or being still to hear His voice. As I learned to
meditate, breathing in God's closeness and love, I awakened to deep gratitude. It was as if every flower bloomed
more brilliantly, every birdsong rang more clearly, and
every wave crashed more comfortingly on the shore.

Today's world seems bent on systematically fragment-
ing our attention, but we don't have to surrender to that.
I've cultivated a handful of deliberate habits that help me
stay present in my own life. If I'm feeling stuck in
my head—disconnected, disgruntled, or discouraged—
I often wash my hands. This simple act, feeling the
water splash against my skin, allows me to reenter the
present moment. It's almost like slipping back into myself in the same way I would slip into my favorite cozy
cardigan. I thank God for clean water, for the soothing
warmth or refreshing cold. That small shift toward gratitude puts me on a new mental path. Tiny rituals of
attention and presence allow me to reengage with a
grateful heart.

Because I'm Irish, I grew up believing that a cup of
tea could solve everything from frostbite to heartbreak.
The very process of making tea, which requires a certain amount of attention, often helps me come back to

the present moment. I also love the idea of taking a time-out when my thoughts are spinning in a million different directions. I can pause, set a one-minute timer, and close my eyes long enough to pay attention to God's presence within me. I can turn my thoughts to gratitude once again.

What about you? In what ways might God invite you to pay attention to your life today? You can start in this present moment with a deep, cleansing breath and a "Thank You" to God. Let's do it together, my friend.

Be an Angel

In the Bible, every time an angel visited Earth, people sat up and paid attention. The presence of angels naturally led people to thanksgiving and praise. Let's take a moment right now to pay attention to one beautiful thing around us—the flicker of a candle, the whistle of the kettle, the scent of that flower. Let's give thanks for that and not stop there!

28

Embrace the Discipline

Gratitude as a discipline involves a conscious
choice. . . . It is amazing how many occasions
present themselves in which I can choose
gratitude instead of a complaint.

HENRI J. M. NOUWEN,
The Return of the Prodigal Son

onday morning call times for *Touched by an Angel* often meant waking up at 3:30 or 4:00 A.M. So much for the glamorous life of an actress! To be ready to film at first light, I often had to brave frigid winter mornings in Utah, where the show was filmed. Bleary-eyed, I'd grab a quick cup of coffee and start the engine of my car, rubbing my hands together briskly. Backing out of my garage, I felt overwhelmed by a single thought: *Thank You, God, for Roy.*

I had hired Roy to plow my driveway after every snowfall. I trusted that he would get to my house— sometimes even before my alarm went off—to clear the road so I could make it to the set. I was so grateful for this man's hard work and faithfulness.

So instead of feeling grumpy or complaining about my early call time, I decided to be thankful. I'm not saying that I loved getting up before dawn. The discipline of choosing gratitude made a difference in me, though. So did receiving mail addressed to Della's and my angel characters, Tess and Monica.

Della and I regularly picked a couple of these letters to read aloud to the cast and crew. It takes an army to make a weekly television program, and sharing viewers' messages of gratitude blessed everyone on set. Pastors wrote, thanking us for illustrations they could use in their sermons. Teachers thanked us for lessons they could teach their students. Perhaps the most moving, however, were the letters from prisoners.

Some told us their stories and sorrows, but most simply thanked us for reminding them that God never stops loving. He never leaves or forsakes *anyone . . . ever.* I can't think of a more appropriate place to broadcast the message of God's never-giving-up, always-and-forever love[11] than within the lonely walls of a prison. I'm so glad the show was there on prison TV sets, week after week.

Some days gratitude comes easily for us. These are the "everyone is smiling and the sun is shining" days. Other days it's not so easy to be grateful, is it? When we're hurt or resentful, being grateful isn't our first reaction. That's why Henri Nouwen called gratitude a discipline.

Discipline isn't spoken of as highly as it used to be. We don't want to have to work at things; we want them to work for us! While this may be understandable, it's not terribly helpful in cultivating a God-honoring life. Doing the daily work of choosing gratitude moves us closer to abundant life.

Whether you are facing another freezing morning commute, find yourself trapped in a dead-end situation, or feel the weight of the world on your shoulders, gratitude is the first and best step closer to the light. And if you feel the sun shining down on you today, why not share that joy with someone else?

Be an Angel

The Bible refers to gratitude well over one hundred times.[12] Seems as though it's an important topic to God! Many of these occurrences involved people thanking God, the Creator and Sustainer of all that we cannot make, do, or maintain. Let's spend some time thanking the Creator of sun and smiles, of you and me. Instead of complaining today when we feel frustrated, we can choose gratitude instead. It's a discipline that will be worth every effort.

Friendship

29

Act Like a Gentleman

The Holy Spirit produces this kind of fruit
in our lives: love, joy, peace, patience, kindness, goodness, faithfulness, gentleness, and
self-control.

GALATIANS 5:22–23 (NLT)

It's been many years since my father passed into
eternity, but I still talk about him frequently. I
often think of how his kindness rippled outward,
touching everyone around him. My dad cultivated im-
peccable manners, down to the habit of tipping his hat
to others as a sign of respect. He dressed, spoke, and
acted like a consummate gentleman. Even more sig-
nificantly, my father was also a gentle man, exhibiting
the fruit of God's Spirit described in Galatians. Growing up, I didn't realize how special this truly was.

As I started my acting career and began interacting
with people from all over the world, however, my
awareness expanded. I understood with greater clarity
how unique my father was, how exceptional *gentleness*
is among men. In an age when it seems that he who

yells the loudest wins, gentleness appears even harder to come by.

Perhaps that's because we mistakenly equate gentleness with weakness. Gentleness certainly isn't prized on the sports field or in the boardroom. If it's spoken of at all, gentleness usually gets relegated to caregivers and quiet places. We may have heard or even believe that gentleness can't get us anywhere or anything.

I know differently because I watched my father live different from most. I know that gentleness is strength under control, a deliberate choice to act honorably and to avoid cruel or severe words. Gentleness is a choice to live like Jesus lived when He walked on Earth.

The original Greek word for "gentleness" used in Galatians 5 means "power with reserve."[13] It's a word that conveys the divine origin of gentleness, emphasizing its inseparability from the character and influence of God. Gentleness "avoids unnecessary harshness, yet without compromising or being too slow to use necessary force."[14] In other words, gentleness is *far* from weak. It knows its own strength and uses it wisely, in the right ways and at the right times. My dad embodied this.

I wonder how different our world might be if gentleness made a comeback. It's pretty clear that the Bible prizes gentleness. "Let your gentleness be evident to all," Philippians 4:5 urges. This isn't a suggestion; it's a command, and God's messengers seem to take it seriously. When angels encounter humans, they don't yell or stir them into a frenzy. They speak calmly and carefully; they act with wisdom, power, and reserve. I believe we can change the world with this kind of gentleness.

Let's start a gentleness revolution—in our families and friendships, on our social media platforms, in our workplaces. We can bring God's message of strength under control to an increasingly uncivil world, just like my dad did. I'm choosing to live that way. Will you join me?

Be an Angel

Take a deep breath and think of someone with whom you have been less than gentle this week. Receive God's forgiveness and grace in prayer. Isn't His love wonderful? Now, what's next? Reach out to the person you snapped at and apologize. Yes, this takes courage. You could come up with a thousand reasons why you can't or shouldn't be the one to seek reconciliation, but this act of humility and love mirrors the work of Jesus and His angels. You can do it, dear one!

30

Hold the Space

My dear brothers and sisters, take note of
this: Everyone should be quick to listen,
slow to speak and slow to become angry.

JAMES 1:19

Whether we're twenty or eighty, a stepparent, a
foster parent, a parent to one, a grandparent
to twelve, or not a parent at all, we can learn from the
children God places around us. In fact, kids probably
act like angels more than most adults do.

My daughter, Reilly, is all grown up now, but God
still uses her to teach me. My beloved girl is an amazing
communicator, and she's helped me develop essential
skills in this area. Some time ago, she began telling me,
"Mom, I just want to say it, not have you fix it" or
"Mom, I just want you to listen; you don't need to
solve this."

Apparently, I had been trying to fix my adult daughter's problems. Or, at the very least, I had been voicing
my opinion about them. Can you imagine?

It's so easy to rush in with our ideas and opinions. It's

especially tempting when we've literally raised a child from birth! Because I don't want Reilly to go through anything hard, I got into the habit of "helping" her with my solutions. However, what Reilly often needs from me—and what she's helped me learn to give her and others—is a loving space to be heard and valued.

In a world where people offer their opinions on anything and everything, choosing to be "quick to listen, slow to speak and slow to become angry" is radical. This is what holding loving space for others means: We let go of our expectations and listen with loving kindness.

It's been said that people will keep telling their stories until they feel heard. Isn't that a striking statement? We all crave someone to really hear us, to create a space that gives us the chance to speak what's on our hearts and minds. After Reilly brought that to my attention, my communication with others grew as a result. My friendships changed beautifully.

Holding a space for others communicates that they are loved and important. This is part of the message that God's angels bring to Earth. Angels remind people of their place in God's story—a significant and honored place. We read a beautiful example of this in Daniel 10:11, when God's angelic messenger declared, "Daniel, you are very precious to God, so listen carefully to what I have to say to you" (NLT). We, too, are precious to God. Every person is. Why not be like an angel, communicating as you listen that the person speaking to you is valued and significant? It will change them—and you.

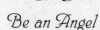

Be an Angel

Listening with God's attentiveness and love doesn't always come naturally. Our human nature pushes us to rush in with opinions or ideas. What do you think about choosing to deliberately hold back your advice unless you're asked for it directly? Try that out and see how being quick to listen and slow to speak might help you be more like an angelic messenger of God's love.

31

Refresh

A sweet friendship refreshes the soul.
PROVERBS 27:9 (MSG)

I'm blessed to have friends I can pick up with anytime, anywhere. In my line of work, when I'm on set or in the throes of developing a production, I may not have time for extended catch-ups or girls' nights out. I can send a quick text or call and say, "Just want you to know I love you and I want to connect soon," but I may not have much more capacity than that. To be able to pick up with a beloved friend after a long absence and feel as if no time has passed is a true gift.

Friends from my school days in Ireland and England, as well as beloved ones from my years in New York City, have endured seasons of tremendous change and challenge with me. These friendships have withstood the tests of time, separation, and distance. I don't take for granted the blessing of friends who refresh my soul; I thank God for them!

I shared a dressing room with one such friend for six

months. We spent hundreds of hours in extremely tight quarters. I remember us laughing and agreeing, "At the end of this, we'll either hate each other or love each other forever." How grateful I am that I have "love each other forever" friends like her. When things are going great, it's such a delight to be reenergized by a friend. And in tough times, when you've forgotten the song in your own heart, a friend can sing it to you.

Friendships in which faith forms the foundation can be especially sweet. One dear friend always finds time to pray with me after a deliciously long conversation. She refreshes my soul! Mark and I also felt the circle of praying friends tightly and lovingly surrounding us during Cameron's illness. Friends restored us in those exhausting weeks at the hospital.

Truly, friendship is a wonderful gift. While acknowledging that, I also want to express that if you are currently lonely or have never experienced the kind of friendship that nourishes the soul, my heart aches with you. Loneliness can be so very painful. I pray that my experiences might encourage you that loving friends *are* out there, even if you haven't met them yet.

Beyond that, I want to invite you to a friendship closer than any other—that is, friendship with God. I've discovered that He is the best of friends. He never fails. He never gives up. He's always loving and true. Like the old hymn proclaims,

What a friend we have in Jesus,
All our sins and griefs to bear!
What a privilege to carry
Everything to God in prayer![15]

Friendship with God truly refreshes the soul. And we can be people who offer that kind of relationship to others. I'm sure you've been around people who frequently complain, focusing on everything that's wrong in the world. We all have moments of struggle and challenge; we don't have to pretend everything is great all the time. That said, it's tough to be with someone whose habit is negativity. So why don't we decide *not* to be a friend like that? Let's refresh the souls of the people we're around. In my experience, an added benefit is that this draws other soul-refreshing people to us. Let's try living like this together.

Be an Angel

When angels interacted with humans, they always pointed people back to God. My praying friends are like this. Let's each be a praying friend for someone else today.

Trust

32

Trust What He Says

Once we deeply trust that we ourselves are precious in God's eyes, we are able to recognize the preciousness of others and their unique places in God's heart.

HENRI J. M. NOUWEN, *Life of the Beloved*

In the devout Irish Catholic home I grew up in, we had a statue of Jesus on our mantel. A lovely image of Jesus also hung in our kitchen on proud display. I genuinely didn't realize—until I was seven or eight years old—that it was a print, not a photograph. I thought we had an actual photo of Jesus!

I attended parochial school and was taught by nuns from my earliest days. I remember daydreaming during one class when I was quite young. While Sister Annunciata talked about Jesus, I gazed out the window. Suddenly, though, she stood directly in front of me, placed her hands on my desk, and gave me her full attention.

"Jesus died for *you,* Roma Downey."

How wretched I felt in that moment! Was it *all my fault* that Jesus died?

Racing home after school, not sure what else to do, I went to the medicine cabinet and located our tube of Germolene. After squeezing the pink-tinged antiseptic ointment onto my finger, I dabbed it on the picture of Jesus. I tended to His hands and feet as well as the wound on His side. I did the same for the statue on our mantelpiece. I loved Jesus so much and wanted Him to know I was sorry. I wanted to make things better.

As you can imagine, my parents wondered what had happened to their picture of Jesus. When I explained what I'd done, they told me Jesus chose to die because I was precious to Him—that it was love that held Him to the cross. Relief flooded my heart. I was precious to God! That knowledge has never left me.

Looking back, I realize how incredibly blessed I was to learn that God is my loving heavenly Father. I'm old enough now to know that not everyone grows up with this understanding. There's quite a bit of confusion about who God is and what He's like. In our modern world, a lot of people think of Him as a harsh judge— a hater, if you will.

I also see so many people who don't believe they are precious; they base their identities on what others think about them. This seems particularly tempting the more time we spend online. There's nothing wrong with enjoying comments and likes, but when our identities rise and fall with how people respond to us, we've left solid ground.

God confirmed the preciousness of every single human when—because of love—He chose to stay on the cross. Jesus was almighty. He could have saved Himself; He chose to save us instead. With His life and death, Jesus declared that we are—*you are!*—precious, beloved, and honored . . . *forever.* I wonder how the world would change if we all chose to trust this truth.

Be an Angel

With what eyes do you look at the world? How do you see others? Do you believe that every person is special and significant to God? Do you trust that you are precious to Him? We all bear the *imago Dei*—the image of God. Let's practice treating everybody we meet today as someone who reflects His precious image.

33

Wait for It

In a garden, growth has its season.
CHANCE the gardener, *Being There*

The 1979 film *Being There* brought the charming tale of Chance, a simple gardener, to the silver screen. Chance spent his life tending the estate of his wealthy employer. Apart from his knowledge of horticulture, Chance learned about the world by watching television. He never left the grounds, never received formal education, never developed life skills. In a bizarre set of circumstances, after his benefactor's death, Chance ends up in the Oval Office, offering insight from the garden that the president interprets as shrewd economic advice: "In a garden, growth has its season. First comes spring and summer, but then we have fall and winter. And then we get spring and summer again."[16]

As a young actress, I loved this movie and its simple, purehearted hero; his care for the earth captivated me. Like Chance, I adore a lovely garden.

When Mark and I married, we moved into a wonderful home and immediately planted a slew of roses around the front and back doors. Then I filled the backyard garden with white and purple flowers, which I'd read promote serenity and balance. To this day, when friends visit, they remark on how peaceful our garden feels. I just love that.

In our garden, one particularly splendid tree grows. Its branches extend like an umbrella, offering shade on warm days. Our family enjoys this tree so much that when we were advised that it needed to be cut back or structurally reinforced, Mark had wooden supports installed. Later, we further strengthened its base, inserting metal in key locations and even adding space heaters. Our beloved tree can now be cool or cozy. We've dubbed it our "Giving Tree," after the brilliant children's book by Shel Silverstein.

Our garden brings me such joy. Its seasons and their cycle require patience, though. I remember Mark asking, "When are we going to see some flowers on those rosebushes?" and our landscaper replying simply, "It takes time, Mr. Burnett."

Growth takes time, doesn't it? And everything has its own growth trajectory.

If you walk from the garden into our home, which we call "The Sanctuary," you may hear the echoes of our children's growth. When we first moved in, they were quite little. Mark and I lined them up behind us choo-choo-train style and chugged through the house, calling out blessings we prayed for our sanctuary. "Peace," I said. "Love," Mark continued. "Joy. Laughter. Refuge." Then the kids jumped in: "Parties! Sleepovers! Peanut butter sandwiches!"

In different seasons, our family has enjoyed all of these. We've experienced winters together too, with loss and heartache. But like *Being There*'s hero, Chance, we've seen that "then we get spring and summer again."

When our children became adults, Mark and I entered a new season. We'd overhear each other on the phone, wheedling with one of the kids to please come home to visit. We wanted them to thrive, but we also missed them terribly. Over time, we relaxed into new rhythms, and we now enjoy that they come home without being asked.

Everything changes with time, and these cycles of growth can unnerve us. But spring and summer always follow fall and winter. Wait for it, friend. A new season is coming.

Be an Angel

In the Bible, angels were never in a hurry. Their sole purpose was to fulfill God's plan, and they did this with focus and patience. Take a few deep breaths and consider if you feel impatient with something. How might you choose to be like an angel and wait for growth and change in a new way? I know how hard that can be, and I'm waiting patiently in my own ways. Let's do it together.

34

Fill Tomorrow

Worry does not empty tomorrow of its sorrow;
it empties today of its strength.
adapted from ALEXANDER MACLAREN,
"Anxious Care"

oes watching or reading the news ever dis-
courage you? If so, you're not alone. Every day
seems to present a new reason for distress. While I'm
writing this book, another violent conflict is unfolding
on the other side of the globe. Children have been
caught in the cross fire, thousands have been forced to
flee, and hatred is exploding along with bombed buildings. This is not what God created people for.

In times like this, I remain informed and active in my
response. I join with others in working toward solutions and peace. I pray wholeheartedly. I also reject the
anxiety that the news can produce in me. While I have
no desire to act as the proverbial ostrich, sticking my
head in the sand, I also know that worry accomplishes
nothing.

Worry empties me. You likely know what I mean.

So why do we do it? Why do we mistakenly believe that worrying about something is better than doing nothing? Anxiety only robs us of peace, steals our joy, and empties today of strength.

That's why I intentionally choose to *fill* my days rather than allowing them to be emptied. Please hear me: I'm in no way advocating that you abdicate your role as a global citizen. We are called by God to love, help, and serve. We are additionally called to fill our minds instead of surrendering them to worry.

So what do I fill my mind and days with? I begin with prayer. I continue with gratitude. I meditate on and seek out beauty. I retreat to nature when I need to reengage my spirit with God's. Fill, not empty. Harmony, not hate. Alleluias, not anxiety. This doesn't happen by accident, dear one. I must choose. You are invited to choose too.

The Bible gives us quite straightforward help in this. Philippians 4:6–7 declares, "Tell God what you need, and thank him for all he has done. Then you will experience God's peace" (NLT). In other words, being thankful is a gateway to peace. I absolutely love that science caught up with God's words a few years ago, when neurologists discovered that it's physiologically impossible to be grateful and worried at the same moment. The neural pathways are mutually exclusive.[17] Isn't that remarkable?

Instead of allowing worry to empty today, we are invited to entrust ourselves to God. We can fill our minds not only with gratitude but with "true, and honorable, and right, and pure, and lovely" thoughts as well (verse 8, NLT). What will you fill tomorrow with, my friend? I'll be awakening the day with prayer and gratitude. I'll choose to fill my mind with truth and beauty, kindness and goodness. Will you join me in this?

Be an Angel

We participate with those around us in emptying or filling their minds. When our conversation continually focuses on what's wrong or worrying, we contribute to the emptying factor. Like angels who bring the message of God's goodness, power, and love to Earth, let's help others turn their problems into prayers today.

35

Put Your Trust

When I am afraid, I put my trust in you. In
God, whose word I praise—in God I trust
and am not afraid.

PSALM 56:3–4

As a child, did you ever wake up from a night-
mare disoriented, unsure what was real and
what was a dream? That was scary, wasn't it? I always
felt awful when one of our children called out in the
dark, awakened by a bad dream. Sometimes I'd hear the
quick padding of small feet down the hall.

"Mom, I'm scared," a little voice might whisper.

Of course, I immediately swept my little one up in a
comforting hug. "It's okay. You're safe. I'm here."

I've also experienced that this is how our heavenly
Father responds when we feel afraid. We need only run
to Him. Isn't that breathtaking?

"What does a little child do when he sees something
that frightens him or confuses him?" Madame Guyon
wrote in the seventeenth century. "He doesn't stand

there and try to fight the thing. He will, in fact, hardly look at the thing that frightens him. Rather, the child will quickly run into the arms of his mother. . . . In exactly the same way, you should turn . . . and *run* to your God."[18]

Fear threatens all of us at some point. It tempts us, in a desperate grab for control, to run to anything but God. But when we pray to the One who made us, loves us, and can help, we come to know we can trust in God and not be afraid.

Psalm 56:3–4 invites us into a circle of sorts. Our trust in God helps us live unafraid, and our understanding of God enables us to trust Him more. So we reach out to God in prayer because we do trust Him, and we trust Him because we know Him. Knowing God and trusting Him are two paths to a place of peace.

Over the course of my life, I've learned to trust God because He shows up, time and again. He is so reliable! Sometimes all it takes to experience peace is the simplest of prayers: "Father, I'm afraid" or "Father, I need You." Other times, fears nag at me. Prayer may not instantly solve things. It always reframes my experience of fear, though.

One of the keys to walking in the trust Psalm 56 describes is making a deliberate mental shift. I choose to place God, rather than my fears, at the front of my mind. By making space for faith and trust, I displace fear. All of us can do this by turning our attention away from fear and focusing on God.

Frightened children want to run to a safe person's arms. Whether or not we grew up with a safe person to run to, we have access to a place of forever safety *now*. God is trustworthy and we can choose Him.

I wonder how different our lives would be if we all chose to keep God front and center in our thoughts. I wonder what our world would be like if we made more space for faith than for fear in our minds and hearts. I'd like to find out. What about you?

Be an Angel

Angels often told people not to fear. With kindness, try speaking that message to your own heart: *Do not be afraid.* Here's a simple prayer you can offer whenever you're afraid: *God, I want to trust in You. Please help me place You, rather than fear, at the front of my mind.*

Grace

36

Receive Grace

What gives me the most hope every day is God's grace,
knowing that His grace is going to give me the strength
for whatever I face, knowing that nothing
is a surprise to God.

RICK WARREN[19]

'm 99.9 percent sure it hadn't happened before and hasn't happened since: Two pastors presented a star to an "angel" on a crowded city street while the Salvation Army band played "When the Saints Go Marching In." I stood, in awe of God and overwhelmed with gratitude, while my name was added to the Hollywood Walk of Fame.

The Hollywood Chamber of Commerce allowed a couple of people to share words on my behalf, so I invited Mark, Pastor Rick Warren, and my beloved friend Della Reese—also an ordained minister—to join me that day. If anyone on Earth was going to tell people what I'm about, I wanted it to be Mark, Della, and Pastor Rick.

Rick and Kay Warren have pastored Mark and me

for many years, and I've known them long enough and closely enough to know they live what they believe. Rick's words about grace come from a well of deep hope and trust in God.

When our son Cameron battled his brain tumor, the Warrens came to the hospital to pray over him and with us. The grace they showed us and the strength they modeled for us were priceless gifts. When their own son's tragic death occurred, Rick and Kay grieved with grace, spoke about mental health with grace, and continued to do the work of God with grace. The Warrens exemplify hope, perseverance, and grace under fire.

In front of a watching world, Rick and Kay have lived out the truth that God's grace gives us strength to face whatever comes our way. They know that serving as pastors doesn't "earn" them grace. Grace is the free gift God offers to all of us, no matter where we've been or where we presently are. The Bible affirms that God's grace saves us. We cannot save ourselves. The Warrens not only teach this but also live it every day. Pastor Rick and Kay are "everyday grace" people, and I'm so deeply thankful for them.

The same day that Pastor Rick spoke words of affirmation over me at the Hollywood Walk of Fame, I also experienced a sad surprise: Della could no longer keep her thoughts and words straight. Age had caught up with her, and confusion had begun to set in. I felt simultaneously caught off guard and protective of my precious friend. But as Pastor Rick pointed out, God was not surprised by Della's situation. His eye was on her, as it always had been. This was a great comfort to me. I knew God's grace would grant Della strength to face what lay before her.

That same grace is a gift available to you and me. Like all gifts, however, it must be received to be of any use or blessing. In Luke 1:28, the angel Gabriel greeted Mary, Jesus' mother, with the ancient Greek word *kecharitomene.* This can be translated "the one given great grace."[20] The angel acknowledged grace as Mary's identity. When Jesus died to save the world, He affirmed that each of us is "one given great grace." I'm wondering, dear friend, if you've received it.

Be an Angel

You can spread the message of grace in a creative way by using the acronym *ANGEL* to describe someone you love. Send your description to them in a lovely card, voice memo, or video. I can attest to how meaningful this can be, as Pastor Rick did this for me. Here's an example:

A . . . Amazing listener
N . . . Nurturing
G . . . Generous
E . . . Encouraging
L . . . Loves lavishly

It doesn't have to be elaborate; just write or record what comes to mind. Added benefit: You'll be blessed as you bless someone else in this way.

37

Live Gracefully

*Grace isn't a little prayer you chant before
receiving a meal. It's a way to live.*
commonly attributed to DWIGHT L. MOODY

*I*n my family, no one would have dreamed of
eating dinner without a prayer of blessing. My
father might lead us in a traditional Catholic prayer:
"Bless us, oh Lord, and these Thy gifts, which we are
about to receive from Thy bounty, through Christ, our
Lord. Amen." Or he might call on one of us to pray, as
he taught us, "from the heart."

Dad taught us to say a prayer of gratitude *after* our
meal as well. Our family bookended every meal with
the remembrance that we didn't get here on our own,
that what we received was a gift of grace, that God always went before and behind us. Dad lived out the Bible's injunction "Whether you eat or drink or whatever
you do, do it all for the glory of God" (1 Corinthians
10:31). Grace wasn't simply a traditional pre-dining
prayer in our home. It certainly wasn't a ritual without

meaning. Grace was a life to be lived . . . a life to be savored.

When Mark and I married, our children felt shy about praying in front of one another. They were new stepsiblings and unsure around one another. Mark and I had decided, as a couple, that we would press through this initial discomfort because family prayer mattered to us. I cannot express how very grateful I am that we persevered. To hear our children, now adults, pray around the table is a priceless gift. Whenever we have guests in our home, we explain our habit of prayer and ask if they are comfortable with our praying grace over the meal. Not one person, even those who don't identify with a faith, has ever said no. Grace is winsome. Grace is lovely. Grace, lived out, draws people toward abundant life.

Grace is, of course, infinitely more than this. The most brilliant theologians have given us metaphors to describe God's grace, but no one can perfectly explain it. Perhaps this is because God intended grace to be lived more than explained.

So how do we begin to live gracefully (i.e., full of grace)? I've found tremendous help in these words attributed to gifted theologian Meister Eckhart: "If the only prayer you ever say in your entire life is 'Thank You,' it will be enough." If grace is the favor of God, given freely (not earned), then gratitude is the most fitting response to that grace in our lives. I want to be grate*full* every day. What about you?

Perhaps you're wondering how this fits with the reality that life is quite difficult. That's precisely why we need grace! It helps us reframe the heartache and turn pain into prayer. Mark and I taught this to our children early on. For example, we could pray for the mean kids at school because we know that hurt people hurt people. Grace doesn't pretend bad things are good; rather, it simply doesn't let bad have the last word.

Living grace*fully* and grate*fully* allows us to love others without conditions. Because we don't have to earn God's grace, we live in grace by not expecting others to earn or perform for our love. That's why the harder life becomes, the more I pray for grace. And I tell you what, dear friend: God always answers that prayer.

Be an Angel

If you or your family doesn't currently have a habit of praying before a meal, why not take this opportunity to start? You can begin with simple thanks for the things you're grateful for and the food you have to eat.

38

Change Gracefully

Grace is the voice that calls us to change
and then gives us the power to pull it off.

MAX LUCADO, *Grace*

race. It frees the spirit. It frees the person. I
know this to be true because, but for God's grace,
my family would have been lost.

After Mom died, we instantly became the canned-
food family. Overnight, I transformed into a latchkey
kid, opening the door to an empty, often cold and dark
home after school. The fire in our kitchen needed to
be lit, and from now on, I would have to do it. I remember standing in the painful quiet, calling out for
my mom.

I also remember needing to help my father arrange
our meals. No Irish dinner is complete without a po-
tato in some form or another, so Dad taught me to peel
potatoes at the sink. Because my father had quite
enough to manage yet still needed his dress shirts
pressed, I learned to iron. I hated being called in from
playing with friends in the street so that I could press

Dad's shirts. Truth be told, I hate ironing to this day. I actually joked with Mark before we married that it was the one chore I simply *don't do.*

What got our family through the massive changes needed after Mom's death? Grace. Every night before bed, Dad, my brother Lawrence, and I would kneel on the linoleum in our kitchen and pray as a family. Praying on linoleum isn't comfortable! But every day, God brought comfort. He answered our prayers: enough strength for that change, that day, that new way of thinking or being. Grief could have consumed us; grace transformed us instead.

We were brought to our knees, but we had Jesus to lean on, and He was enough.

When confronted with the need to change or a prompting to try something different, we often feel tension. Fear of the unknown may creep in (that's perfectly natural!). But if we trust God's grace to empower and change us, we won't be paralyzed by the fear. We have a Bible full of His promises of grace to strengthen us.

Grace describes the character of God; it's part of His fundamental nature. Grace is also the power and influence of God, which has real, practical results in our lives. Grace saves and inspires us, emboldens and equips us. It lifts us above circumstances.

It's amazing what we can do when we must. God made the human spirit remarkably strong. Because of

His grace, we are more resilient than we can possibly imagine. When I reflect on this, I think of Jesus' mother, Mary—how humbly and gracefully she responded when visited by the angel Gabriel. She said yes to a massive life change, and her yes changed the world. But that wasn't the end. Mary continued to say yes to the transforming work of God through the life of her son.

Every yes to God is empowered by grace. Every yes changes the world. What yes is God inviting you to today?

Be an Angel

Take some moments to quietly reflect on what yes God is inviting you to today. Form your thoughts into a prayer and listen for His response. Remember to look for God's grace as you say yes. Depending on the circumstances, He may gently coax, lovingly push, or simply reach out His hand that you might grab hold in faith. In whatever way His grace comes, it comes with power. God's grace does not disappoint. Next to your prayer, write the ways you see His grace supporting you.

Loss

39

Help Someone Heal

[The LORD] heals the brokenhearted and
binds up their wounds.

PSALM 147:3

I love that God is a healer. He longs for us to live
whole and well. He tends to our wounds and
comforts us in heartache. Psalm 147:3 is such a healing
scripture for anyone who's been hurt, had their heart
broken, or experienced any kind of illness or pain. In
other words, this truth is for us all: We are never alone
in our pain.

Like you, I've felt the sorrow of loss. I've been
wounded. I've needed healing and protection. Because
I experienced deep losses and heartache during childhood, I wanted to guard my daughter, Reilly, from everything that might hurt her. I felt this way about my
stepsons, James and Cameron, too. I didn't want any of
my kids to suffer. Perhaps you have loved someone like
this, loved them so much that you'd do anything to
prevent heartbreak from reaching them.

Because my own mom died just before my tenth

birthday, I worried about death more than other healthy young mothers did. I'm so very grateful that Reilly didn't have to endure what I did as a wee girl. But I couldn't protect her from every wound. The truth is, the people we love need God even more than they need us. He is the only one who completely "heals the brokenhearted and binds up their wounds." He can heal your heart too.

One of the first significant losses that Reilly and I shared happened when Della went to be with Jesus. Della was far more than a colleague; she was even more than a friend. She was a second mother to me, and a grandmother to Reilly. Her warmth and love formed part of the fabric of our lives. When Della passed, we felt so devastated, but God comforted us in our heartache.

One astonishing thing about faith is that the more we lean into God in times of loss, the more we experience His love. He holds us up and holds us together. I know this is true because I have experienced it. I've watched it in the lives of others. The reverse can also be true: The less we lean into God for comfort and healing, the deeper our wounds go. Healing is available, but like all gifts, it must be received to become fully our own.

My father once shared the Margaret Fishback Powers poem "Footprints" with me. It relates the story of one person's journey, represented by footprints in the sand. The narrator sees God's footprints alongside his own but expresses confusion at the single set of foot-prints visible during the most troubling and painful times in his life.

"Why would You leave me when I needed You most?" he asks God.

My precious child, the Lord responds, *I never left you. When you saw only one set of footprints, it was then that I carried you.*[21]

Most of my adult life, I've carried credit-card-size copies of "Footprints" to give to others. God always seems to bring someone across my path who needs the words of hope and encouragement: *I love you. I will never leave you. I will carry you when you hurt the most.* God puts words like these in the mouths of His mes-sengers, the angels. They are words He can put on *our* lips too. Let's receive God's healing for our hurts and help others heal as well.

Be an Angel

Thinking about hurt and loss can feel heavy. Take a moment to meditate on God's healing love. Now let's turn to others. Is there someone brokenhearted around you right now? What small act of kindness can you do, or what words of hope might you be able to speak? You can help someone heal through God's presence in you.

40

Be Defined By . . .

> You may not control all the events that hap-
> pen to you, but you can decide not to be
> reduced by them.
>
> MAYA ANGELOU, *Letter to My Daughter*

aving my father read poetry to me every night before bed was a comforting ritual I look back on with fondness. I can still hear his voice bringing to life the words of Irish poets like William Butler Yeats and Seamus Heaney.

I grew up, but I never outgrew my love for poetry. In fact, I developed an even deeper respect for the skill it takes to communicate the human experience through words. In adulthood, I read Maya Angelou's poetry and identified with it profoundly. Maya understood loss and heartache, things I learned early in my childhood, with my beloved mother's untimely death.

None of us escapes suffering. None of us gets through life unscathed. The sadness of this reality could reduce us, but it doesn't have to. The words of singer-songwriter Leonard Cohen expand on this truth: "There is a crack, a crack in everything," but "that's how the light gets in."[22] We all need angel messengers to remind us of this truth and to help us press into light and love.

I recently watched a fascinating television program about the development of character in visual storytelling. The narrator described how villains often suffer a defining loss that leaves visible evidence: perhaps an ugly scar on their face or an unsightly limp.

Heroes, too, usually experience a defining loss. They may have been orphaned, suffered a terrible illness, or been treated cruelly by others. The strength and wisdom heroes manifest come not despite their losses but often because of them.

Villains allow defining losses to reduce them, but heroes accept their losses as pathways to strength. Their wounds become the places where light enters. Heroes don't want anyone else to suffer as they have, and they work to prevent heartache in the world.

What story do your losses tell, dear one? What scars do you bear? No one lives without loss. No one avoids heartbreak. The question is, How will we respond to our wounds?

I find it fascinating that after Jesus rose from the grave, His scars remained (see John 20:24–29). He easily could have done away with the physical reminders of His suffering on the cross. Instead, His scars will tell the story of His heroism throughout all eternity.

The Bible tells us that angels also have stories of conflict and warfare (see Daniel 10:13–21). God's messengers can relate to our battles, yet they still brought God's messages of love and light. And—whatever life throws at us—we can too.

Be an Angel

Reading about loss may bring up difficult memories for you. Please breathe with me, taking in God's love and exhaling the pain of the past. Imagine an angel coming to you and listen for God's voice: *There is healing and forgiveness with Me. Let go of this wound. I can help you bear it. Some people use their free will to hurt others, but pain will not have the last word. I will never leave you, because I love you.* As you rest in the assurance that God is always there for you, I'll be doing the same.

41

Look Inside

(In my sleep I dreamed this poem)
Someone I loved once gave me
a box full of darkness.
It took me years to understand
that this, too, was a gift.

MARY OLIVER, "The Uses of Sorrow"

I hated seeing him hurt. He's such a remarkable young man, my stepson: thoughtful, loving, and true. That day he was quite heartbroken over a recent and painful breakup. I listened quietly, letting him process. I remembered Mary Oliver's poem "The Uses of Sorrow" and gently shared her meaning. "Please trust me: Someday you'll be able to look back on this in a new way."

I could say this only because I have experienced it. When I first encountered Oliver's poem, I wept. Life had already given me several boxes full of darkness, and it took me years to understand that they, too, can be gifts. I've lived long enough to realize that, through every circumstance, a blessing can come.

I know what it's like to look into the darkness. Everything within us wants to reject it. But if we can reach beyond, we eventually see and experience breakthrough. I trust in time, a great healer, and in Jesus, the Great Healer.

At several points in my career, I felt crushed by disappointment. I was sure I'd get this role or that opportunity, but I didn't get every job. One role in particular I wanted so badly. I'd had a schoolgirl crush on my potential co-star for years and was so excited about the possibility of working with him (and really, who *doesn't* love Kevin Costner?!). When I didn't book the part, a slew of doubts slithered into my mind. Only in retrospect could I see that this box of darkness was really a gift: If I hadn't been turned down for that role, I never would have had the chance to combine the work I love with my faith in God on *Touched by an Angel.*

Life hands us all boxes of darkness, doesn't it? Mary Oliver's evocative words touch on every loss, every betrayal by a friend, every heartache in our families, every cruel word spoken to us. Our trust is broken, our joy is stolen, and negative emotions can fill us with brooding darkness.

When it happens, I remind myself, *This too shall pass.*

Pain. Disappointment. Rejection. *These too shall pass.*

When we face loss, it's difficult to see downstream. We can't envision the turns life will take, how pain might eventually lead us to a gift we can't imagine. We're simply invited to trust. I know this is difficult, especially when we are newly heartbroken or when we have been hurt repeatedly for many years. But do you want, one day, to take the box of darkness down, look inside, and see what kind of gift it is? I know you do.

The angel who appeared to Jesus' mother, Mary, brought great news and also a box of darkness. In the ancient world, Mary would have experienced scorn and shame for a pregnancy others couldn't understand. The gift of her son Jesus and His gift to all the world through death and resurrection were worth the heartache. Yes, the pain was real, but so was the blessing. This truth is our truth too.

Be an Angel

Imagine an angel has come to you, ready to look with you at your own boxes of darkness. Choose one memory and allow God to show you what He's done to bring light from this loss. Breathe in His presence, and then invite and receive His healing.

Encouragement

42

Dance

Nobody cares if you can't dance well. Just get up and dance. Great dancers are not great because of their technique; they are great because of their passion.

attributed to MARTHA GRAHAM,
Time magazine's Dancer of the Century

*P*osting Friday dance videos online has been a tradition of mine for some time now. I love clips of professionals at the top of their game, elderly couples whose passion for dance spreads the best kind of infectious joy, or tiny dancers giving it their all with no reference to technique.

Encouragement—that's what my posts are about. I find dance videos that bring me joy and I share them with everyone in my sphere. I want to encourage people, as renowned American dancer and choreographer Martha Graham did, to discover dance as "the hidden language of the soul."[23]

Sometimes words fail us. We need a language beyond, a language that taps into the depth of emotions or experiences we may not be able to process cognitively. And yet, all too often, we're reluctant to let loose; we're too self-conscious to dance.

When I was quite young, my mother enrolled me in Irish-step-dance and ballet classes. Truth be told, I wasn't brilliant at either, but I enjoyed the classes tremendously. I have vivid memories of being in a crowd of tutus and eager children, scanning the room for my mom. There she was, watching lovingly and attentively, encouraging me with a small nod as if to say, *Good on you, my girl. I'm here.* Her encouragement gave me the confidence I needed to pursue my dreams.

Fast-forward many years, and I'm married to Mark, who, although quite good at dancing, often expresses reticence to get on the floor. I'll lovingly coax (and, if necessary, finagle) until he joins me. After a while, both of us are laughing. The joy is so freeing! When we sit down, spent from the fun, he almost invariably says something like "I forgot how much I enjoy dancing."

We forget so many of the things that bring us joy, so many of the things that encourage our hearts. We think we're being watched or evaluated all the time, so we're hesitant to let go and allow the songs of our bodies to break forth. I've lived long enough to know that Martha Graham was right: Nobody cares if you're a great dancer. Indeed, other people are usually too worried about themselves to think about you at all.

What song does your body need to sing? What does

your soul need to say that words cannot express? The Bible tells us that when he was overwhelmed with joy, King David "danced before the LORD with all his might" (2 Samuel 6:14, NLT). Whether we are completely able-bodied and can dance freely or we have physical limitations, all of us can dance with joy in some way, even if all our might includes only the smallest of movements. Today is a great day to dance into the rest of our lives.

Be an Angel

True confession: I'm a secret salsa dancer! The track "Despacito" gets me on my feet every time! So does ABBA's "Dancing Queen." What one song makes you want to move? Put it on as loud as you dare and dance around in whatever way you're able to enjoy. Don't stop until the last note sounds. Notice how you feel, and then form your thoughts into a prayer. Like an angel would, turn to God with grateful joy.

43

Soar

Where there is no struggle, there is no strength.
attributed to OPRAH WINFREY

*I*t's no secret that I love butterflies. I wear butterfly jewelry. I buy butterfly art. I titled my first book *Box of Butterflies*. I love these remarkable creatures not simply because of their beauty but also because of what they symbolize.

Shortly after my mother passed into eternity, my father and I brought pansies (Mom's favorite flower), which she thought resembled tiny butterflies, to plant by her graveside. As Dad and I stood on the breezy hillside praying, a butterfly flew right in front of us, dancing on the wind. God used that butterfly, and He has used butterflies ever since, to comfort and encourage me.

Over the years, I've visited butterfly houses and observed eggs, caterpillars feeding on leaves, chrysalides in various stages of formation, butterflies emerging from chrysalides, and—most magnificent—fully formed butterflies soaring around and above me. In every good butterfly house, a guide will explain the harrowing journey of the caterpillar that wraps itself in darkness and emerges only through terrific struggle to soar in the light.

In the butterfly's case, Oprah's words are quite literal. The very act of wrestling against the tightly woven chrysalis strengthens the butterfly's wings. A butterfly prematurely released from its chrysalis cannot fly. Instead of marvelously buoyant wings, the butterfly who hasn't struggled suffers from a withered body and shriveled wings that are unable to support its weight.

Without the struggle, there is no strength. Our hearts resonate with this truth—and recoil from it at the same time. We don't *want* this to be true. We yearn for a soaring-all-the-time life, not one in which darkness cocoons us, pain transforms us, and beauty follows suffering.

When we're young, one of the reasons heartache and loss hurt so dreadfully is because we are experiencing darkness for the first time. We have not yet lost and found joy again. We have not yet suffered a broken heart and come out on the other side. However, as we age and grow, we remember that others have risen. We ourselves have risen. We gain strength from that truth. We will rise again, whether the darkness is lengthy or mercifully short.

Some years ago, on Valentine's Day, Mark took me

outside to our patio and handed me an exquisitely designed box crowned with a fragrant gardenia. I had no idea what the box held. Its weight gave no indication. Smiling, my husband told me to open it carefully, so I gently removed the lid. Out flew fifty butterflies. Gasping, laughing, crying, grateful, I watched in wonder as they ascended into the sky, a soaring reminder of God's presence and grace. It was the dearest gift I've ever received.

In the years since, we have sent boxes of butterflies to others, encouraging them to remember that strength solidifies in struggle, that darkness breaks into light, that God—in all His glorious beauty and splendor—will never leave or forsake us. "In this world you will have trouble," Jesus proclaimed. "But take heart! I have overcome the world" (John 16:33). Because He has overcome, we can too. Look to the butterfly, dear one, and be encouraged.

Be an Angel

Visit a butterfly exhibit or watch a video on butterflies. Look for the powerful and hopeful truths God wrote into these amazing creatures. Consider sending a box of butterflies to someone (or to yourself). Enjoy the joyous soaring of these remarkable creatures, and embrace your own soaring strength!

44

Build Up

Encourage one another and build
each other up.

1 Thessalonians 5:11

I take encouragement seriously. There are enough
critics in the world; I want to build people up.
Inspiring others with faith, love, and light is the thread
that holds my whole career together.

Mark and I formed our production company, Light-
Workers Media, with the express purpose of encouraging people. We create content that brings hope and life
to the world. LightWorkers celebrates the good all
around us, reminding us that God's grace is unshakable,
His love unmistakable, and His kindness contagious.

There are plenty of forces in the world that try to
tear people down, but we don't attack them; we simply
build up instead. At our company, we often quote the
popular axiom "It's better to light a candle than to curse
the darkness."[24]

Back when we needed to choose a name for our
production company, we came up with a million ideas.

It was far more difficult than one might imagine to name a company with intentionality. There were a couple of names we really liked, but we'd attempt to register them and find out they were taken. Ugh!

Eventually, God brought us to just the right name. Jesus tells us that He is the Light of the World (see John 8:12). We are His workers. And so LightWorkers' name and purpose solidified. We work to bring light; we build up others because *everyone* needs encouragement.

No matter how successful someone is or seems, they want to know that their work is seen and valued. People also want to be known and cherished for who they are, not just what they do. I'm no exception to that rule! Mark has been such an encourager in my life, and I endeavor to be that for him. We both pay attention to the details of each other's lives and offer encouraging feedback. My daughter, Reilly, has become such an amazing encourager as well. She's usually the first one to send me a text appreciating something I've done: "Great work, Mom" or "I'm so proud of you." I can't express how much this means to me.

When things aren't going smoothly in our own lives, in our country, or on the world stage, it may feel easier to be a critic. But I've discovered that it drains me to be negative or to disparage, to shame or to critique. Research shows this to be true for others too.[25] Conversely, encouraging others strengthens us rather than drains us.[26] It's a win–win situation. When we build up others, we feel built up as well. So, dear one, which will you choose to be: a critic or an encourager?

Be an Angel

Remember that angels are God's messengers. What would being a messenger of encouragement look like in your life? Are there things you're currently doing that you may wish to add to, change, or cut out? Today is a great day to start.

Joy

45

Release the Shout

Inside everyone is a great shout of joy waiting to be born.

DAVID WHYTE,
"The Winter of Listening"

*M*y brother Lawrence taught me to whistle.
As a wee girl, I could manage only reverse
whistling: that half-musical sound made while sucking
air in. But one day I found my whistle, and I've been
unstoppable ever since.

When I read David Whyte's poem "The Winter of
Listening," I immediately identified with his shout-of-
joy image. I sincerely believe my whistle comes from
the joy God placed inside me. It's released sometimes
deliberately, sometimes unintentionally, but always with
delight. Whistling is the music of my heart.

We sometimes hear people use the words *joy* and
happiness interchangeably. While there's certainly cross-
over, I've come to understand joy and happiness as
unique experiences. Happiness, I've discovered, in-

volves my external circumstances. It's quite dependent on situation; joy, on the other hand, is an inside job.

I see this in my ninety-two-year-old mother-in-law, Jean. Despite the challenges of growing older, Jean retains a joyful spirit. Her delectable sense of humor remains firmly intact. She celebrates the little things. She still walks her beloved dog, Frank. And she always looks forward to time with family. Recently, I told Jean I'd be visiting her in England and had planned a fancy luncheon for us. Her reaction? "What am I going to wear?" Even at ninety-two, she wants a fabulous outfit. I just love her. No matter what's going on around Jean, her joy remains strong.

Historically, when angels visited Earth or revealed glimpses of heavenly glory to humans, shouts of joy accompanied them. In Luke 2:13–14, delighted exaltation poured from God's angelic host. Isn't it good to know that angels aren't always serious? In fact, they're often rather exuberant. As God's created and beloved children, why should we live any differently?

I believe we connect most deeply with whom God created us to be when we release the unique shouts of joy He's placed within us. My whistle, Jean's humor, my daughter's gorgeous singing voice—there's a shout of joy in every child of God. That includes you.

Perhaps you already know what your shout of joy feels, looks, or sounds like. Maybe it's the amazing quilts you craft, the enchanting stories you tell, the rich melodies your instrument produces as you play. Or it could be the powerful words you write, the exquisite meals you cook, the way you selflessly serve others. Our shouts of joy are distinct and personal.

Some of us, through a painful past or the hurtful words of others, have silenced our shouts of joy. I'm so sorry if this is your experience. I pray that today you would begin to release your joy. It may come out quietly at first, but look forward to the day that it will be a shout of exclamation mirroring God's heavenly host. Come, dear one: It's time to shout.

Be an Angel

We can encourage those around us to release their joy even as we let loose the shouts of joy within us. Your encouragement may be the very thing someone needs to overcome the insecurity or fear they feel. Whose joy can you help release this week? Be on the lookout, my friend, and help that person discover their unique shout of joy.

46

Live Again

George has been kicked out of six retirement homes. . . . He's angry, he's unhappy, he's old, and it's my job to help him find the joy in living again.
MONICA, *Touched by an Angel*

They started with a bald cap. Next came the liquid latex, applied in thin layers. Using a blow-dryer, makeup artists crafted deep wrinkles on this second skin, then commenced with a paint job mimicking the translucence of old age and the pigmentation of age spots. A white candy-floss wig crowned my head. Over a few hours, I aged fifty years.

In the episode "Missing in Action," my character needed to be transformed into an elderly woman in order to take on a tough case: a cantankerous old veteran named George. To help her stop seeing George as old and needy, God transforms Monica into an elderly woman, placing her undercover as a resident in George's retirement home.

I was thirty-six years old when I filmed that episode, and the magnificent makeup artistry that turned me into an eighty-six-year-old woman did more than transform how I looked on television; it also revealed how differently the world sees people based on age. If you ask me, our society is quite ageist, especially when it comes to women. Can I get an amen?

Growing old is treated almost like an illness in the prosperous Western world, where people focus on "fixing" wrinkles, sagging skin, and age spots. For a woman *not* to be discontented with her appearance seems almost odd in this day and age. It's expected that women will want peels and treatments, creams and solutions. Too many of us don't want to be ourselves; we'd rather be young, whatever the cost.

When Monica went undercover to serve George as his angel caseworker, becoming old wasn't a punishment. It was an opportunity, an invitation. Monica had essential lessons to learn from those in the retirement community. They had gleaned tremendous wisdom over time and had valuable things to teach and share. If we're consumed with trying to defy aging, we can miss the significant gifts that people with extended years on Earth can offer.

The Bible mentions age in reference to only one angel, the "young man" at Jesus' tomb (Mark 16:5). When it comes to God's heavenly host, age apparently matters so little that the other roughly three hundred occasions on which the Bible mentions angels contain no indication of it. What matters is their wisdom and purpose. I wonder what it would be like if we all lived as if those things—not our age or appearance—were the most important facets of our identity.

I realize that we live in a visual world. I won't be giving up makeup or moisturizer, my friend, and I'm not asking you to either. I'm only asking that we consider what matters *most*. I enjoy looking nice, but what's most important is who I am, revealed in what I do, say, and believe.

Filming "Missing in Action" provided me the opportunity to look into the future—to see what I might look like in fifty years. I'm also grateful that, through this episode, God invited me to investigate my heart. This entry is an invitation for you to look within and entrust God with everything: your age, identity, and purpose. Why not take a few moments to do that right now?

Be an Angel

How can we treat those with age and experience with greater honor and respect? Perhaps you can be like an angel by listening to someone whose advanced years have afforded them wisdom and insight. If you're willing, I trust God will give you the opportunity.

47

Be Complete

I have told you this so that my joy may be in
you and that your joy may be complete.

JOHN 15:11

*I*t's quite an astounding promise: Fullness of joy
can be ours. Jesus told the disciples this during
their final meal together, commonly called the Last
Supper. They had gathered in an upper room for the
Passover. A short time later, Jesus would die. According
to the Bible, Jesus' promise to make His joy in us complete was among the final words He spoke on Earth.

While filming *The Bible* miniseries, we paid special
attention to the upper-room scene. It became an incredibly intimate and even holy experience for all of us on
set. The room we chose for the scene felt almost cave-
like, ancient and close. In most cases, considering the
limited amount of space, a producer might wait somewhere else and review the footage later. But I had promised Diogo, the actor who played Jesus, that I'd walk
with him through every scene. I told him this before I
agreed to take on the role of Christ's mother, Mary.

While filming the Last Supper, I folded myself into a small corner so as not to disturb the shoot, and I prayed continuously. Despite the seriousness of the scene, God brought a joy that united everyone there. His Spirit truly filled that space.

In the upper room, Jesus hooked His promise of joy to the phrase "I have told you this." It came directly after He explained why being close to—"abiding in"—Him is so very important. The biblical word *abide* connotes the idea of being at home in or with God.[27] If we stay near Jesus, at home in and with Him, joy and love flow from us, filling our hearts and spilling over into the lives of everyone around us.

While promoting *The Bible,* Mark and I saw this happen in incredible ways. In Hollywood, it can be quite difficult for Christians to lead with their faith. There are many expectations and false assumptions about religion, so it often takes people some time to open up about their faith. *The Bible* miniseries became a bridge people could walk across, a way for them to speak about their relationship with God. An elevator attendant here, a receptionist there, a driver taking us to our next promo event—they'd thank us or talk to us about their faith journey or their experience watching the show. As I obeyed God's call to bring His story to life onscreen, I felt even closer to Him. What a blessing that was! Abiding in this way brought me such joy, and I was reminded—as I had been during my years on *Touched by an Angel*—that I could help others draw closer to God by being loving and bold with my faith. How wonderful!

What a privilege to show others how to enjoy closeness with God. An incredible added benefit is that as the joy of Jesus is made complete in us, there is less room for negative emotions like worry, anger, and bitterness in our minds and hearts. Let's not wait to experience greater joy; let's draw close to God and allow Him to make our joy complete.

Be an Angel

Remember, Jesus' words about abiding and joy were some of His last. If you could plan your own last words, what would they be? What message would you want to send to the people you love right before you went home to heaven? Like an angel, speak that message with joy.

Change

48

Fix the Flat

A bad attitude is like a flat tire.
If you don't change it, you won't go anywhere.
attributed to JOYCE MEYER

No one wishes for a flat tire, and no one deliberately chooses to drive with one. In fact, we universally feel aggravated by them. Perhaps that's why Joyce Meyer's comparing a bad attitude to a flat tire strikes me so powerfully.

I encountered a flat-tire moment recently. With a team of incredible colleagues, I'd been working long hours to bring a remarkable tale of hope to the big screen. Based on a true story, the movie required significant special effects to realistically portray what occurred. Getting the news that we'd exceeded our special-effects budget (and in no small way!) felt like a kick in the gut. I could almost hear my attitude deflating like a blown tire.

In that moment, choices confronted me. Would I wallow? Would I blame? Would I take my frustration out on someone else? Or would I pause, shift my perspective, and look for a solution? I knew that, because I was a lead producer, my response would affect not only me but also the whole team. I'd help or hinder the entire film with my attitude.

Thankfully, my dad taught me early in life that, for every problem, there is a solution. He may have allowed me a short wallow when I was young, but he always pointed me forward. I felt free to express frustration, but I also learned not to let it control me. Somewhat like patching a flat tire, Dad helped me exchange a deflating attitude for a solution-oriented one.

I passed this same lesson on to my daughter and stepsons. In fact, to this day, Reilly will finish my statement: "For every problem . . ." I'll start. "There is a solution," she'll respond. Solution-oriented thinking isn't simply a way to avoid frustration; it also empowers us to move forward, not just simply to stay away from flat tires.

In the Bible, angels often showed up when people had run out of options. Genesis 18 records one such encounter. God had promised Abraham a son, yet twenty-five years later, he and Sarah still had no children. At age ninety-nine and eighty-nine, respectively, they likely felt that their biological clocks had stopped altogether. In this seemingly impossible situation, three angels showed up, bringing God's message of hope and life: "You *will* have a son" (see verse 10).

Sarah's attitude was—how can I say this nicely?—a bit flat-tire-ish. She actually laughed. The angel of the Lord inquired about her laughter, and Sarah—understandably, from a human perspective—tried to cover up her bad attitude with a lie. God was not fooled. He pressed in, helping Sarah change her flat-tire thinking. In fact, He did such a miraculous work that Sarah named her son Isaac, which means "laughter." The New Testament later commends Sarah as a woman of faith (see Hebrews 11:11), reminding us that no matter how bad our attitude may be in a particular moment, God can change everything.

Be an Angel

Angels may not manifest themselves to you like they did to Sarah, but God sends His messages in a myriad of ways. Why not take this opportunity to consider how an angel would evaluate your recent attitude? Sometimes we don't realize how flat our tires have become! When we're not going anywhere and we feel frustrated, what we may need is a change of perspective. Pause with me, dear one. Listen to your mind and heart and determine whether a change of attitude would help you find the solution for a problem you're facing.

49

Make a Habit of It

> You will never change your life until you
> change something you do daily. The se-
> cret of your success is found in your daily
> routine.
>
> JOHN C. MAXWELL, *How Successful People Grow*

Leadership guru John Maxwell's books have sold millions of copies. Once named the world's number one leadership expert, Maxwell has a thing or two to say about success. He is also a committed person of faith, and his words about the importance of daily habits can be easily applied to our journey with God.

I really identify with something Maxwell empha- sizes: Success isn't accidental; diligence and practice matter. True, some people receive natural gifts that en- able them to reach great heights. Yet even folks with tremendous blessings don't reach their potential by chance.

Two of the most decorated athletes of all time—Tom Brady and the late Kobe Bryant—demonstrated this. Both had been given extraordinary physical gifts. Their bodies seemed created for maximum performance. But neither Brady nor Bryant rested on their innate talents. Teammates report that they got to practice early and stayed late, working in the off-season, pushing themselves continually. No matter how people felt about either player, no one could impeach their work ethic and commitment. Both athletes cultivated habits of discipline and daily routines that propelled them forward.

I feel fortunate that my dad instilled homespun wisdom about diligence and success in me. "Proper preparation prevents poor performance" was one of Paddy Downey's favorite sayings. Even through a simple task like folding laundry, Dad would emphasize, "How you do anything is how you do everything" or "Anything worth doing is worth doing well, Roma." Those lessons could have annoyed me, but I chose to receive them instead. I learned that cultivating habits of excellence would set me apart.

I began cultivating daily habits early in my acting profession, routines that kept me sharp and disciplines that paid huge dividends as my career grew. I put in long hours and committed myself to excellence, no matter how small the part. I took classes and worked diligently on my accents (especially since some jobs required me to drop my native Irish lilt and some required that I pick up another accent altogether). I memorized scripts so that I could perform rather than read—also known as being off-book—during auditions. Habits like these formed me.

We can also integrate daily habits into our journey of faith. We can make a habit of spending time with God. That way, when He speaks, we know His voice because we're familiar with it. We're not simply asking a stranger to do something for us; we're in fellowship with the One who loves us and will never leave or forsake us (see Deuteronomy 31:6). How wonderful is that?

Jesus' mother, Mary, gives us an excellent example of this. When the angel Gabriel announced the good news to Mary, she was ready to receive it. She answered, "I am the Lord's servant. May everything you have said about me come true" (Luke 1:38, NLT). God's angelic messenger found Mary prepared. Most likely we won't receive a supernatural visit like this, but we can make it a habit to be ready in every aspect of life: professional, personal, and, most importantly, spiritual. If an angel came to you, would God's messenger find you ready?

Be an Angel

What one change can you make in your daily routine? Consider starting a habit of daily gratitude or carving out time for prayer. Perhaps you'll feel led to make a practical change at work. Remember, life change begins with daily change. Let's change together, dear one.

50

Be For, Not Against

The journey changes you; it should change
you. It leaves marks on your memory, on
your consciousness, on your heart, and on
your body.

ANTHONY BOURDAIN, *No Reservations*

The air was heavy with spices. Mark and I were
traveling in India, and every sight, smell, and
color felt exotic. Years before, I had been captivated by
the film *Gandhi*. Watching the life of this remarkable
man touched me deeply. I thought, *Someday I want to
experience India.*

Now here I was, in a minivan, surrounded by daz-
zling saris, the pungent scent of curry and saffron, and a
teeming crush of humanity. As our driver slowed at an
intersection, a man on the side of the road caught my
eye. He swung a pickax forcefully, fracturing the ground
blow by blow. Standing and leaning back with a hand on
his hip, the man stretched to relieve the soreness from
such backbreaking labor. He turned, and I saw his face
for the first time, only it wasn't a man; it was a woman.

Had I been born in a different nation or at a different time, that could have been me. I didn't know how to process my emotions. I felt wretched—*What am I supposed to do about this?*—then quickly I felt ashamed that I wanted to give her something, when, from all appearances, she was simply doing an honest day's work. The memory left its mark.

Mark and I traveled on to Varanasi, considered the most sacred city along the Ganges River. Pilgrims come from near and far to pray, ritually bathe, and attend to their dead. Some come to Varanasi to die. Once again, the sensory overload was difficult for me to process. People bathed in the Ganges not far from others washing their laundry, while others, only a short distance away, scattered the ashes of loved ones whose bodies had been cremated that very day. It was all so raw and real, so very human.

Later that night, a guide took Mark and me on the Ganges in a small boat. With other vessels gathered around, we released tiny candles on the water. This ritual, we learned, allowed all of us who attended to remember those we had lost, those we had loved, and those who had gone before—ancestors we never knew but whose lives shaped our own.

In India, I encountered a profound oneness with humanity. We all love and lose. We have families and dreams. We work and wash and live and die. I learned that we can understand one another's pain if we open ourselves to it. There is hope for our world if we choose to see people as more like us than different from us. Our perspectives can shift.

In one biblical account, an angel appeared to Joshua, a religious and military leader. With a drawn sword, the angel blocked Joshua's way.

"Are you for us or for our enemies?" Joshua asked.

"Neither," the angel replied, "but as commander of the army of the LORD I have now come" (Joshua 5:13–14). The angel was *for* God, not against others.

I wonder how our world would change if, like this angel, we rejected us-versus-them thinking. What if we lived less *against* things and people and more *for* what unites us: being made in the image of God? I'd like to find out. What about you?

Be an Angel

Take a moment to consider if there is someone or something you're being called to see differently. How might you shift to being *for* rather than *against* others?

51

Start with You

Be the change you wish to see in the world.

GANDHI[28]

When it came to backgammon, Della Reese had the edge on me. During long breaks on set, she tutored me—then mostly defeated me—in round after round of backgammon. I loved those times, even if I never mastered the game as magnificently as she did. Our conversations while playing ranged from hilarious to monumental. There's never been someone quite like Della.

One day, she peered at me with that intense gaze of hers. "Listen to me, angel girl. Pay attention when something bothers you. There's a lesson there."

"What do you mean?" I asked.

"When people annoy us, the very thing we don't like about them is often something we don't like about ourselves."

I immediately sensed the truth in what Della shared, and it brought to mind Gandhi's words about change, which I had heard years before. His words are true on the global stage. We can change the world only by starting with ourselves, altering one thought at a time, one action at a time, one decision at a time. After I spoke with Della, it also occurred to me how true Gandhi's words are on the small stage of my own life. The very things that bother me in *that* person might be what I need to alter in *this* person: me.

So I started looking at what irks me, considering what I'd want changed, then doing for someone else what I'd want done. I get up early and make tea for Mark. I reach out to that colleague and say sorry for being short with her. I speak life into the world with what I create, do, and post. *Be the change, Roma,* I can almost hear Della whisper.

We can't change everything, but we can work toward peace when we change ourselves. We're better able to participate in the fight against injustice when we're released from our own internal wars. If we don't attend to what's inside, we simply don't have the bandwidth to be the change on a grander scale.

In the book of Judges, an angel appeared to God's people, confronting their misplaced priorities. They had abandoned God and "did whatever seemed right in their own eyes" (17:6, NLT). When the angel spoke, the people wept at what was revealed (see 2:1–5). Unlike the Israelites, we don't have to wait for an angel to appear and show us how we need to change. We can take the initiative and willingly open our hearts to change. What do you think?

Be an Angel

Take a deep breath and consider . . . What is one thing you've been waiting for someone else to change? How might you change first? Why not try that instead today?

52

Be an Angel

I could not have made it this far had there not been angels along the way.

DELLA REESE

*D*ear one, we've come to the end of our journey together. Thank you for sharing this time with me, reflecting on faith, love, and trust. Thank you for considering what it's like to be a messenger of God. I've loved working on this book, and I pray you've enjoyed reading it.

As we close, I'm thrilled to give Ms. Della Reese the final word. I love reflecting on how she was like an angel to so many, including me. She always emphasized God's love and truth.

Della was filled with such faith and joy—and a whole lot of sass to go with it. She experienced a lot of pain too. As a Black woman who endured segregation and racism for many years and in many ways, she faced odds others may have found insurmountable. She trusted God and overcame.

Della refused to accept the limits others tried to place

on her life. She lived like a warrior angel and inspired not just me but so many others as well. And because Della looked for God in everyone and everything, she saw God everywhere. Angels were all around her. God sent Maya Angelou to be like an angel in Della's life. She and Maya had endured many of the same hardships. They encouraged and sharpened each other. They spoke the message of God, reminding each other of His presence and power.

Della was very much like an angel in my life. She helped me learn to trust God more: "Baby, when you've prayed about something, you don't have to keep asking God over and over. You can tell Him, 'Thank You for handling this, Lord. I trust You.'" That was just one of the many messages of truth Della spoke into my life.

Then one tragic day, I was able to be an angel for Della. Her daughter died suddenly, and I was able to rush Della to the airport, fly back to Los Angeles with her, and deliver her to the loving arms of her husband. In those moments, I hardly spoke; I simply held my beloved friend's hand and prayed for her. Later, I was able to be like an angel to Della as she neared the end of her life. It was such a privilege to love her in this way.

Sometimes we need an angel, and sometimes God asks us to be like an angel. That's what this book is about: tracing God's fingerprints in our lives, deliberately cultivating ways we can be part of His plan and work. Because these things take practice to implement, I encourage you to go back and put into action some of the "Be an Angel" encouragements that were especially helpful or challenging for you.

Thank you again, dear one, for taking this time with me. I pray that, no matter where you started, your relationship with God has grown, that you have allowed yourself to be folded in the wings of His angels, and that you feel His loving embrace every day of your life.

Be an Angel

What is God nudging you to do today? When He encourages us to be kind or loving, to offer forgiveness or let our joy loose, let's not wait one minute! May each of us be like an angel in someone's life today.

Acknowledgments

A special thanks for the loving support of my marvelous book agents, Shannon Marven and Jan Miller at Dupree Miller, the true angels in my journey as an author. I also am so grateful for their incredibly hardworking team members, Sydney Keith and Rebecca Silensky Echols.

A special thanks to my publishers, Becky Nesbitt and Tina Constable, for believing in this book from the very beginning. I also appreciate the insightful input from the rest of the very talented team at Penguin Random House/Convergent: Steve Boriack, Rachel Tockstein, Linnea Knollmueller, Jocelyn Kiker, Sally Franklin, Jo Anne Metsch, Jessie Bright, and Leita Williams. Their work helped deliver a beautiful book, and I am so grateful. Thank you, everyone!

I am supported in every possible way by the hard

work and attention to detail of my LightWorkers team, so special thanks to Chanshi Chibwe, Janet Perez, and Brittany Burkett. Thanks also to Brian Edwards for his wisdom. I am so very grateful for Jerusha Clark and the love and light she brought to help me shape these stories so prayerfully and joyfully. Last but certainly not least, I so value my team at Frank PR. Clare Anne Darragh and Lina Plath are my warrior angels who walk beside me.

And to all the angels along the way who arrived as friends and family to love, support, and encourage me: You know who you are, and I thank each of you from the bottom of my heart.

Notes

1. Serge-Thomas Bonino, "Renowned Angel Expert Explains Amazing Facts Every Catholic Should Know about Angels," interview by Solène Tadié, *National Catholic Register,* September 29, 2020, ncregister.com/blog/angels-101.
2. Dictionary.com, s.v. "angel," dictionary.com/browse/angel.
3. "Who Is St. Nicholas?," The St. Nicholas Center: Discovering the Truth about Santa Claus, stnicholascenter.org/who-is-st-nicholas.
4. "Saint Nicholas Day (Mikuláš)," My Czech Republic, myczechre public.com/czech_culture/czech_holidays/saint_nicholas.html.
5. Joan Graff Clucas, *Mother Teresa* (New York: Chelsea House, 1988), 35.
6. "Peter R. Scholtes, 1938–2009," Peter Scholtes, pscholtes.com /obituary.htm.
7. Father Scholtes's original lyrics included this line: "We'll guard each man's dignity and save each man's pride." Over the years, more inclusive adaptations such as the one used in this book— "We'll guard each other's dignity and save each other's pride"— became popular.
8. "Mark Burnett on the Miniseries *The Bible:* More Than Half the People Alive Will Probably See It Eventually," Yahoo! Entertainment, August 23, 2013, yahoo.com/entertainment/blogs/emmys

/mark-burnett-on-the-miniseries--the-bible--more-than-half
-the-people-alive-will-probably-see-it-eventually-233243821
.html.

9. William Butler Yeats, "The Lake Isle of Innisfree," Poetry Foundation, poetryfoundation.org/poems/43281/the-lake-isle-of-innis
free.

10. See Max Lucado, *He Still Moves Stones: Everyone Needs a Miracle*
(Nashville: Thomas Nelson, 1999), 92.

11. Sally Lloyd-Jones, *The Jesus Storybook Bible: Every Story Whispers
His Name* (Grand Rapids, Mich.: Zonderkidz, 2007), 36.

12. Jonathan McAnulty, "Thanksgiving Important Theme in Psalms,"
Gallipolis Daily Tribune, November 12, 2015, mydailytribune.com
/opinion/3007/thanksgiving-important-theme-in-psalms.
    See also Christina Dronen, "Gratitude in the Bible—Key Verses
and How to Apply Them," Gentle Christian Parenting, March 8,
2021, gentlechristianparenting.com/gratitude.

13. "4240. Prautés," Bible Hub, biblehub.com/greek/4240.htm.

14. "4236. Praotés," Bible Hub, biblehub.com/greek/4236.htm.

15. Joseph M. Scriven, "What a Friend We Have in Jesus," 1855, public domain.

16. *Being There,* directed by Hal Ashby, Lorimar, 1979.

17. Dan Baker and Cameron Stauth, *What Happy People Know: How
the New Science of Happiness Can Change Your Life for the Better*
(New York: St. Martin's, 2003), 81.

18. Jeanne Guyon, *Experiencing the Depths of Jesus Christ* (Sargent, Ga.:
SeedSowers, 1975), 85.

19. Pastor Rick Warren, Facebook, October 29, 2015, facebook.com
/pastorrickwarren/posts/what-gives-me-the-most-hope-every
-day-is-gods-grace-knowing-that-his-grace-is-go
/10153665628940903.

20. Charles Grondin, " 'Full of Grace' Versus 'Highly Favored,' " Catholic Answers, catholic.com/qa/full-of-grace-versus-highly-favored.

21. The "Footprints" I grew up with was paraphrased from Margaret
Fishback Powers's poem google.com/books/edition/Footprints
/lzTIOifmWGsC?hl=en&gbpv=0 (1964). Powers is one of several to claim authorship of this poem. See poetryfoundation.org
/articles/68974/enter-sandman.

22. Leonard Cohen, "Anthem," *The Future,* Columbia Records, 1992.

23. Martha Graham, "Martha Graham Reflects on Her Art and a Life in Dance," *New York Times,* March 31, 1985, nytimes.com/1985 /03/31/arts/martha-graham-reflects-on-her-art-and-a-life-in -dance.html.

24. The first iteration of this quote has been traced to William Lons-dale Watkinson, "Sermon XIV: The Invincible Strategy," in *The Supreme Conquest, and Other Sermons Preached in America* (New York: Revell, 1907), 218, books.google.com/books?id=U4sOA AAAIAAJ&q=%22candle+than%22#v=snippet&q=%22candle %20than%22&f=false.

25. See Bree Maloney, "The Damaging Effects of Negativity," Marque Medical (blog), marquemedical.com/damaging-effects-of-nega tivity.

26. See "Kindness Matters Guide," Mental Health Foundation, men-talhealth.org.uk/campaigns/kindness/kindness-matters-guide.

27. See Andrew Murray, *Abide in Christ: The Joy of Being in God's Pres-ence* (New Kensington, Pa.: Whitaker House, 1979); and Witness Lee, "Abiding, Dwelling, and Making Home in Christ," in *The Secret of Experiencing Christ,* originally published 1986, minis trysamples.org/excerpts/abiding-dwelling-and-making-home-in -christ.html.

28. Gandhi's actual words have been altered over time. He originally said, "We but mirror the world. All the tendencies present in the outer world are to be found in the world of our body. If we could change ourselves, the tendencies in the world would also change. As a man changes his own nature, so does the attitude of the world change towards him. This is the divine mystery supreme. A won-derful thing it is and the source of our happiness. We need not wait to see what others do." This has become "Be the change you wish to see in the world." The original quote comes from Mahatma Gandhi, "General Knowledge About Health XXXII: Accidents; Snake-Bite," in *The Collected Works of Mahatma Gandhi,* vol. 12, *April 1913–December 1914* (Delhi: Publications Division, Ministry of Information and Broadcasting, 1964), 158; see quoteinvestigator .com/2017/10/23/be-change.

ROMA DOWNEY is an Emmy-nominated actress, producer, and *New York Times* bestselling author who has been creating inspirational content for twenty-five years. Best known for her role as the kindhearted angel Monica on the popular network show *Touched by an Angel,* Downey is the founder and creative head of LightWorkers, the faith and family division of MGM. Their productions include *The Bible* miniseries, *A.D.: The Bible Continues, Son of God, The Dovekeepers, Woodlawn, Ben-Hur, Resurrection,* and the upcoming film *On a Wing and a Prayer.* As part of her 2021 birthday list, Queen Elizabeth II bestowed Downey with an OBE for services to the arts, to drama, and to the community in Northern Ireland. Downey is a longtime supporter of Operation Smile and Compassion International, and she received a Sally Award from the Salvation Army for her contributions to entertainment and her commitment to helping those in need. She was also honored for her career with a star on the Hollywood Walk of Fame. She and her husband, Mark Burnett, live in California. They have three amazing children and three wonderful dogs.